Politics Over Process

Although the U.S. Constitution requires that the House of Representatives and the Senate pass legislation in identical form before it can be sent to the president for final approval, the process of resolving differences between the chambers has received surprisingly little scholarly attention. Hong Min Park, Steven S. Smith, and Ryan J. Vander Wielen document the dramatic changes in intercameral resolution that have occurred over recent decades, and examine the various considerations made by the chambers when determining the manner in which the House and Senate pursue conciliation. *Politics Over Process* demonstrates that partisan competition, increasing party polarization, and institutional reforms have encouraged the majority party to more creatively restructure post-passage processes, often avoiding the traditional standing committee and conference processes altogether.

Hong Min Park is Associate Professor of Political Science at the University of Wisconsin—Milwaukee.

Steven S. Smith is Kate M. Gregg Distinguished Professor of Social Science, Professor of Political Science, and Director of the Weidenbaum Center on the Economy, Government, and Public Policy at Washington University in St. Louis.

Ryan J. Vander Wielen is Associate Professor of Political Science and Associate Professor (by courtesy) of Economics at Temple University.

LEGISLATIVE POLITICS & POLICY MAKING

Series Editors

Janet M. Box-Steffensmeier, Vernal Riffe Professor of Political Science,
The Ohio State University

David Canon, Professor of Political Science, University of Wisconsin, Madison

POLITICS OVER PROCESS

Partisan Conflict and Post-Passage Processes
in the U.S. Congress

Hong Min Park, Steven S. Smith,
and Ryan J. Vander Wielen

University of Michigan Press
Ann Arbor

Published in the United States of America by the
University of Michigan Press
Manufactured in the United States of America
♾ Printed on acid-free paper

2020   2019   2018   2017   4   3   2   1

A CIP catalog record for this book is available from the British Library.

Library of Congress Cataloging-in-Publication data has been applied for.

ISBN: 978-0-472-13051-1 (hardcover : alk paper)
ISBN: 978-0-472-12318-6 (ebook)

Contents

Figures

Tables

Preface

In 2008, while the Senate was considering a supplemental appropriations bill, Senator Thad Cochran (R-MS) addressed the Senate to express his regrets about how a bill he favored was being considered by the House and Senate. Cochran had been in the Senate for nearly three decades by then and had served as chair of the Committee on Appropriations. He observed:

> I am . . . concerned that the process by which Congress will consider the supplemental will again be through a series of messages between the House and the Senate. The House will neither hold a committee markup nor generate an original bill for consideration. As such, it appears there will be no conference committee to reconcile differences between the House and Senate. Rather, the committee leadership, as well as the majority leadership in the House and Senate, will retire behind closed doors to produce a final product for our consideration. The minority will be part of the discussion to varying degrees, but there will be no conference meeting to attend, there will be no conference votes to decide items of disagreement, and there will be no conference report for Members to sign or not to sign.
>
> None of these procedures are without precedent. The Republican majority at times employed similar tactics to move legislation. But I fear that in the appropriations realm, we are making a habit of these procedures–a bad habit. Processing bills by exchanging messages with the House is becoming the norm rather than the excep-

tion. Formal conference committees are becoming rare. It seems that committee markups may be the next part of the regular order to go by the boards. This trend should be of concern to all Members of the Senate, not just the members of the Appropriations Committee. (*Congressional Record*, April 24, 2008, S3387)

Cochran was observing a trend that involved more than appropriations bills, although appropriations bills were a central part of the story. Since the mid-20th century, Congress experienced two waves of change in the use of conference committees to resolve differences between the House and Senate. The first wave, a product of changes in the structure of the legislative agenda and the expectations of House Democrats, reduced the number of bills going to conference but increased the number of legislators appointed to conference committees. The second wave, which we associate with the election of a Republican majority in the 1994 elections, initiated a sequence of events that led to a dramatic decline in the use of conference committees and more frequent use of ping-pong methods (exchanging amendments between the houses) and other innovative approaches.

This monograph is about the causes and consequences of these changes in the way relations between the House and Senate are managed. Our story is a vital part of a larger story about the changing political environment in which Congress legislates—or often fails to legislate. The story involves the effects of partisan and factional battles on the procedural strategies employed by parties and leaders. These partisan and factional battles have changed character and so have the strategies of the parties. One result, the near evaporation of conference committees, is a surprise to many observers and a disappointment to many members of Congress. We explain why.

We dig into the history of House-Senate reconciliation methods in recent decades, but we also marshal a large body of data about post-passage methods. We bring to bear a complete account of all members in all conferences since 1963 and present ancillary data on the parent committees, parties, and chambers. We also benefit from the considerable efforts of many of our colleagues in political science who have documented and coded a remarkable range of congressional activities and behavior.

Collecting these data would not have been possible without the financial support of the Weidenbaum Center at Washington University in St. Louis and the dedicated research assistants who worked closely with us. Our assistants include Jessica Karlow, Dustin Palmer, Mark Plattner, Miriam Ben Abdallah, Nay'Chelle Harris, Michelle Shapiro, Stephanie Burdrus, and Kaleb Demerew at Washington University and Lauren Erdman,

Mackenzie Merry, and Sean Sullivan at the University of Alabama. Thank you. We also thank our colleagues at the Weidenbaum Center—Melinda Warren, Gloria Lucy, and Christine Moseley—for their assistance.

The politics of House-Senate relations is important. Process affects outcomes. We have chosen to write this monograph to highlight the most important ways in which House-Senate relations have evolved in recent decades. We hope that our efforts will inform serious discussions of how Congress does and should conduct its business. We also hope that our discussion motivates our political science colleagues to dig deeper into the relationships among politics, process, and policy that we introduce here.

ONE

Fundamental Change in Post-Passage Politics

Most observers of congressional politics are surprised to learn that in the 113th Congress (2013–2014), Congress enacted 296 public laws but only three of them—about 1 percent—involved a conference committee to resolve differences between the House and Senate. In contrast, in the 95th Congress (1977–1978), 143 of the 633 public laws, or about 23 percent, were enacted after a House-Senate conference completed the details. Over those four decades, conference committees, which were once considered basic features of congressional action on major bills, all but evaporated.

In figure 1.1, we report on the percentage of enacted public laws in each Congress that were taken to conference to resolve differences between the two chambers of Congress. Beginning in the late nineteenth century, conferences assumed a prominent role in lawmaking. In fact, most major legislation was approved after a conference committee recommended a final version of the measure. A conference committee includes a delegation appointed by each chamber, usually the senior members of the House and Senate committees in which the legislation originated. The process was considered an extension of the committee system and was run by the chairs of the committees.

Something happened. Actually, several things happened in congressional politics that led party and committee leaders to choose alternative methods for bringing the House and Senate into formal agreement on the language of legislation. As we will see, a committee-oriented legislative process was replaced by a party-oriented process, which eventually under-

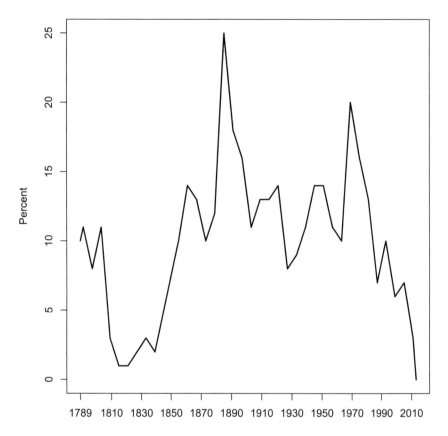

Fig. 1.1. Percentage of public laws going to conference, 1789–2014. (Rybicki [2003, 2007] for the period 1789–1962, and data collected by the authors from *CQ Almanac* for the period 1963–2014.)

mined the value of going to conference. This book is about this revolutionary change in how the two chambers of Congress interact with one another and its consequences for legislative outcomes.

Some Basics

Although the Constitution requires both chambers of Congress to pass identical versions of a bill before legislation can be sent to the president, it is silent with respect to the procedures that Congress employs to reconcile legislative differences. The House and Senate avoid the need to resolve differences when one chamber simply approves the bill initially passed by the other chamber. This is the most common method for completing the legislative process. Remarkably, for bills that become law, this path is used about three-quarters of the time. These tend to be simple or minor bills and sometimes involve informal coordination among legislators and committees before the legislation is passed.

When one chamber passes the other chamber's bill with amendments, the chambers must then determine a way to resolve their differences. Most modern mechanisms for resolving these differences and the rules governing their use were introduced during the nineteenth century (Rybicki 2003), and the rules and precedents governing these mechanisms are now well established and extensive.

The most common mechanism for resolving intercameral differences is for one chamber to accept the other chamber's amended version (Oleszek et al. 2016). While it is often the most efficient method, exchanging amendments between the houses can be a lengthy process because it can be continued for multiple stages. At each stage, a chamber can decide to make multiple further amendments, concur in some or all of the other chamber's amendments, or disagree to some or all of the other chamber's amendments, and then send the legislation back to the other chamber.[1] Of course, the amendments can be entirely new proposals that generate more debate and controversy. This back-and-forth process is called "an exchange of amendments" or, more informally, a "ping-pong" process.

For important and complex legislation, the number of differences between the chambers can be large and quite difficult to resolve. Rather, lengthy and more interactive negotiations may be required. Conference committees, composed of a delegation of legislators appointed by each chamber, have been used to structure such negotiations. A majority of conferees from each chamber must approve the conference agreement (called a "conference report"), which then returns to the chambers to be considered by a single up-or-down vote in each house.[2] The conference report must be approved by each house before a bill can be sent to the president for her or his signature. In the mid-twentieth century, the number of conferences was about twice the number of ping-pong efforts for measures requiring reconciliation of House-Senate differences.

In contrast to standing committees and floor politics in each chamber, post-passage politics have received little scholarly attention. Of the work exploring questions relating to post-passage politics, the primary focus has been conference committees, and, in particular, determining which chamber has an advantage when bills go to this reconciliation process (Steiner

1951; Fenno 1966; Vogler 1970; Ferejohn 1975). But we know very little about the individual and collective behavior of members at the post-passage stage. For example, when do party leaders encourage the use of conferences to reconcile intercameral differences, and how has this changed over time? What is the preference composition of conference committees, and how does this affect the policy outcomes they produce? Given that the post-passage stage is the last point at which the details of most legislative measures are modified, different types of conciliation mechanisms may have significant implications for the policies that emerge from Congress.

The objective of this book is to explore the considerations of the chambers when deciding how to resolve intercameral differences. As we later show, there has been considerable variation across both time and issues in how the chambers resolve these differences, yet the existing literature provides few insights regarding the chambers' decision calculus at this stage of the legislative process. This book seeks to fill this gap in the literature by providing a theoretical account that identifies the key determinants of change in post-passage strategies, and offering a historical examination of intercameral resolution in the U.S. Congress, with particular attention given to the role played by congressional conference committees. In addition, we offer an exploratory analysis of the policy consequences of this historical pattern.

Overview of Conference Committees

At the heart of the bicameral system is the necessity for compromise between chambers.[3] Needless to say, this can prove to be a difficult task, as the chambers are collectively populated by 535 members who represent constituents with a wide array of interests. One means of reconciling differences between the House and Senate is the congressional conference committee. Conference committees are by no means an innovation introduced by the American system, though. The roots of conference committees date back to fourteenth-century England (Longley and Oleszek 1989). Records indicate that the burgeoning parliament had used conference committees as early as 1378 (Tiefer 1989). Moreover, conference committees were a prominent means of reconciling intercameral conflict in the early English system.

Since the colonial governments drew much of their inspiration from the English model, conference committees were adopted as a conciliation mechanism in many colonial legislatures (McCown 1927). Given the role that conference committees played in the colonial legislatures, which had important influences on the design of the U.S. Congress, the almost immediate use of conference committees in the early U.S. Congress was quite natural. On April 17, 1789, following a conference to prepare the rules that would govern the use of future conference committees, the House followed the Senate's lead and agreed to a resolution that put into place in both chambers the first rules for conference committees (Longley and Oleszek 1989). The resolution read:

> Resolved, That, in every case of an amendment to a bill agreed to in one House and dissented to in the other, if either House shall request a conference, and appoint a committee for that purpose, and the other House shall also appoint a committee to confer, such committee shall, at a convenient time, to be agreed on by their chairman, meet in the conference chamber, and state to each other verbally, or in writing, as either shall choose, the reasons of their respective Houses for and against the amendment, and confer freely thereon. (Ibid., 30–31)

Institutional Importance

Since the first Congress, conference committees have undergone a considerable evolution. The rules and procedures governing conferences have changed substantially, as have the norms surrounding conferences. In addition, the frequency of the appointment of conference committees has varied widely across time, which, we will show, is a by-product of important changes in the role of standing committees and legislative parties in House and Senate decision making. To better understand the role that conferences have played throughout the history of Congress, we begin by examining the frequency of their use, and the significance of the legislation that goes to conference. Although the policy implications of the mechanism have yet to be explored, it is reasonable to expect that higher rates of conference usage increase the opportunities for this mechanism to play an influential role in shaping policy outcomes. And, furthermore, we would likely conclude that conference committees have greater influence if the legislation that typically goes to conference is important.

Figure 1.1 offers some insight into the frequency with which conferences have historically been used. There is considerable fluctuation in the use of conference across time. The Congresses preceding the Civil War were generally characterized by minimal use of conference. However, following the marked increase in the use of conferences in the decades leading up to the Civil War, Congress, on average, relied upon conference to a much larger extent until the most recent Congresses. Approximately 14 percent of all public laws enacted between the end of Civil War and the end of the twentieth century went through conference (Rybicki 2003). This is particularly impressive when one considers the fact that the vast majority of public laws enacted do not involve any conflict between the chambers.

Also impressive is the frequency with which important legislation historically has been sent to conference. To be sure, conference committees are used to resolve conflict on legislation of various degrees of importance. Nevertheless, there is strong evidence that important legislation has a greater likelihood of going to conference. Figure 1.2 presents the percentage of important measures resolved in conference, using two different methods for classifying legislative importance. The first method uses a coding scheme developed by Mayhew (1991, 2005). The method requires that legislation receive attention in the annual roundup stories of the *New York Times* or *Washington Post*, or both, as well as receive in-depth coverage in the *Congressional Quarterly Almanac*.[4] Using this data series, an average of approximately 75 percent of important legislation went to the conference stage between 1945 and 2010, with 100 percent of important legislation going to conference in some Congresses. The second method for identifying important legislation includes all legislation receiving at least 125 column lines (i.e., the median number of column lines) of coverage in the *Congressional Quarterly Almanac*. This method generates a considerably larger population of important measures than Mayhew's method. Nevertheless, the aggregate trends are consistent across these measures, and the second method likewise points to an extremely high probability of important legislation going to conference. Over the period of 1963 to 2010, roughly 58 percent of important legislation was resolved in conference using this measure of importance.

We can conclude from this brief, introductory overview, which is discussed in far more detail in the chapters to follow, that throughout most of the post–Civil War era conference committees have historically played an active role in legislating. Plainly, conference committees have been the dominant method of resolving House-Senate differences for most important legislation since the mid-nineteenth century until recent decades. Both houses had committee-oriented policy-making processes so it was natural for them to rely on their committee leaders to resolve inter-cameral differences. In recent decades, that method for handling major legislation is no longer standard. There has been a stark decline

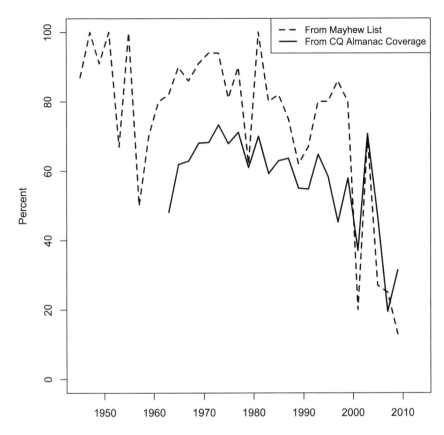

Fig. 1.2. Percentage of important legislation going to conference, 1945–2010. (Rybicki [2003] and David Mayhew's website (http://campuspress.yale.edu/ davidmayhew/datasets-divided-we-govern/) for the Mayhew list, and Policy Agendas Project for the *CQ Almanac* coverage data.)

in the use of conference committees to a point that one might even conclude that their role in legislating is, at best, trivial. *Why is that the case?* We seek to answer this question below. Before doing so, however, we briefly review what others have said about conference committees in the scholarly literature and elsewhere.

The Political Science of Post-Passage Decision Making in Congress

While research on post-passage politics has been somewhat limited, there have been essentially four lines of inquiry: (1) Which chamber wins when measures are resolved in conference? (2) Are conference committees composed of preference outliers? (3) Do conference committees produce biased policy outcomes? and (4) What factors influence the chambers' decisions regarding post-passage politics? While we characterize the literature in these four strands of research questions, it is important to note that they are not mutually exclusive categories. Work on conference composition and influence, for example, plays an important role in the more recent conversations about the decisions made by the chambers regarding post-passage resolution. The motivations of conferees, and their influence on policy outcomes, is logically related to the considerations made by party leaders regarding which methods of intercameral resolution they pursue.

A considerable amount of the early scholarly literature examining conference committees was dedicated to determining whether the outcomes of conference committees reflect a greater influence of one chamber over the other (Steiner 1951; Fenno 1966; Vogler 1970; Ferejohn 1975). This area of research resulted in a variety of conclusions regarding which chamber has an advantage in conference, with most arguments suggesting that institutional differences between the chambers contribute to unequal bargaining positions in conference. Therefore, this literature assumed that the chambers themselves possess certain advantages when going to conference, irrespective of any characteristics relating to the members appointed to negotiate.

The literature dedicated to explaining "who wins" in conference adopted the conventional assumption that conferees go to this conciliation process with only the interests of their parent bodies in mind. These studies were rooted firmly in notion that "individual legislator's convictions are expected to be subordinated to the larger purpose of obtaining a conference bill similar to his chamber's bill" (Vogler 1970, 87). Moreover, the language of this assumption permeated the early conference literature. After all, it is not uncommon even today to encounter descriptions of the conference process that suggest that conferences are a means of "splitting the difference" between the chambers or a simple "give and take" between the chamber positions (Longley and Oleszek 1989; Vogler 1970). Yet this assumption was based on little more than the idea that conferees are "supposed" to represent the views of the parent bodies. However, scholars soon began to question whether this assumption was a fair characterization of the autonomy of conferences. In other words, work prefaced on this assumption precluded the important possibility that conference committees are independent actors in the legislative game.

During the early scholarly discussions about conference committees, there had been few efforts to examine conferences that relaxed this assumption, thereby permitting the possibility that conferees pursue their own interests at this stage in the legislative process. This was a particularly important consideration since the preferences of conferees are not necessarily compatible with the preferences of the chambers. Shepsle and Weingast (1987) critique the "who wins" literature, stating:

> The evidence . . . suggests an even more persuasive reason for doubting the relevance of this question ["who wins?"]. The conference may be less an arena for bicameral conflict than one in which kindred spirits from the two chambers get together to hammer out a mutually acceptable deal. Surely on some (many?) subjects . . . the members of the House and Senate (sub)committees who control the conference have more in common with one another than either may have with fellow chamber members. (101)

Consequently, scholars have begun to examine the conference appointment process (Carson and Vander Wielen 2002; Hines and Civettini 2004; Lazarus and Monroe 2007; Vander Wielen and Smith 2011). Like Shepsle and Weingast, many of these studies conclude that preference outliers frequently dominate conference committees. Vander Wielen and Smith (2011), for example, find evidence of majority party bias in the selection of conferees in the House, but less conclusive evidence of conferee bias in the Senate, consistent with differences between the chambers in terms of the powers afforded the majority party in the conferee selection process. The driving force behind exploring the subject of conference composition is to better understand its implications for policy.

However, examining conference committee composition alone is not adequate for the purposes of assessing the policy implications of conferences, since we cannot assume that preference outliers will necessarily pursue their *own* interests. Such an assumption would be as constraining as the assumption made in the "who wins" literature that conferees will inevitably represent their parent bodies. While the presence of preference outliers on conference committees may be a necessary condition for policy bias, it is certainly not sufficient. Instead, this was a call for scholars to more directly examine the relationship between the ideological composition of conference committees and policy outcomes. While scholars had provided some anecdotal evidence linking biased conference committees to policy outcomes that deviate from the wishes of their parent chambers (e.g., Nagler 1989), the role that conferees play in shaping policy outcomes had been given little theoretical or empirical scrutiny.

Perhaps the earliest work to theorize about the influence of conferees on policy outcomes is the *ex post* veto literature. In Shepsle and Weingast's (1987) seminal article, the authors contend that members of Congress have adopted a norm of deference to committees because of the access that committee members have to conference committees. In conference, members are able to modify the given legislation and offer their alternative to the chambers for vote under closed rule. The ability of conferees to choose any policy outcome that is at least as preferred by the chamber to the status quo often renders opposition to the committee's preferences futile according to this argument. Shepsle and Weingast, therefore, posit that the pivotal position that committee members have in the legislative process, via conference committees, creates the appearance that rank-and-file members are deferential to the preferences of committees. This work suggests that rank-and-file members acknowledge the capability of conferees to bias policy outcomes in their favor and, as a result, typically do not expend valuable resources to amend legislation that comes from the parent committee.

While the *ex post* veto model is not without its critics (e.g., Krehbiel 1987; Smith 1988), Shepsle and Weingast contend that conference committees are extended important institutional protections that allow them to pursue biased policy outcomes. Following this lead, Vander Wielen (2010) examines the extent to which conferees pursue their own policy preferences, perhaps at the expense of the parent chambers. Proposing a theoretical model in which conferees are independent actors (of the parent chambers, as opposed to the conventional perspective of conferees as faithful agents of the chambers), he identifies spatial (i.e., ideological) arrangements of the chambers and conference delegations that provide a test of the policy influence of conference committees.[5] He finds evidence that conference committees systematically move policy away from the parent chambers toward their preferred policy locations—a finding that is inconsistent with the notion that conferees solely pursue the interests of the chambers from which they come. In later work, Vander Wielen (2012) argues that the chambers are willing to incur this policy cost to reduce the risk of bargaining failure between the chambers, given that conference committees have certain informational advantages. Ryan (2014), examining conference committees at the state level, similarly finds evidence that conference committees have a meaningful and predictable influence on policy outcomes. In particular, in states that permit the minority to propose an alternative to the conference report, conference committees produce more moderate policies, which again points to variation in policies that should not occur if conferees are exclusively motivated by the interests of their parent chambers.

The final strand of the literature, which to date has received scant attention, addresses the dramatic decline in conference committees that we noted in figure 1.1. The few studies that have examined this recent phenomenon point to partisan polarization and minority obstruction as important determinants of the diminished use of conferences in recent Congresses (Ryan 2011; Sinclair 2012a). These studies provide important first steps toward answering an important, and complicated, question that has considerable implications for the policies that emerge from Congress. In the pages to follow, we forward a theoretical model that posits a role of these, and other, factors in explaining the ebb and flow of conference use across time. We suggest that it is a more complicated story than the ones presented by the existing studies that overlook several intertwined additional factors.

Theoretical Accounts

The political science of post-passage politics offers few insights into why we see such dramatic change in the use of conciliation methods across time. Here, we offer a theoretical story to explain the observation that the one-time common conference committees have all but disappeared. We start with the observation that congressional parties exist to achieve their members' electoral and policy goals. The parties and their leaders pursue the collective goals of gaining or retaining majority party status and enacting policy that reflects their members' common policy objectives. Party members may differ in how they define these collective goals, and they certainly may differ over strategies for pursuing them, but these collective goals are important enough to unite members under a common party label to pursue collective efforts.

We contend that there are three central, and overarching, factors that cause variation in how congressional parties define and pursue their collective goals: (1) the competitiveness of parties, (2) the distribution of policy preferences both within and across the chambers' parties, and (3) inherited institutions. To be sure, other contextual factors certainly contribute to the decisions made by the chambers regarding which post-passage method to use at any point in time, but these three factors, we argue, are the most central determinants.

Partisan Competition

A motivating goal of congressional parties is to gain or retain majority party status. After all, majority party status bestows considerable institutional advantages on majority party members that better situate them to attain their electoral and legislative goals. Yet there is considerable variation across time in terms of the demands on the majority party (minority party) to retain (attain) majority party status in successive Congresses. Figure 1.3 offers some very basic insights into this point by presenting the proportion of two-party seats held by the Democratic Party between 1937 and 2016. For instance, in the 75th Congress (1937–1938), there were 75 Democrats and 16 Republicans, which means that the Democrats enjoyed a whopping 59 seat advantage, or roughly 83 percent of all the two-party seats in the chamber. It is probably reasonable to assume that the Democrats were not kept awake at night with concerns about losing their majority in the following Congress. However, more recent congressional majorities may not have slept so soundly.

In periods of great uncertainty about majority status, parties have a strong incentive to devote more resources to electorally beneficial activities and often expand the organizational capacity when they are electorally insecure (Smith and Gamm 2009, 2013; Gamm and Smith forthcoming; Lee 2016). As we observed, the 1980 election of Ronald Reagan to the presidency and a Republican majority in the Senate brought a long-term period of intense interparty competition for control over the major policymaking institutions of the federal government (Gamm and Smith forthcoming). Uncertainty about long-term control of a chamber of Congress, which rises when party control is more fluid (i.e., as the lines in figure 1.3 more frequently cross the 50 percent line), forces parties to invest more in well-known electoral strategies like public relations, messaging, credit claiming, and blame attribution. Few major issues are approached in the modern era without regard to their electoral consequences. While some issues are more vital to a party's national reputation, the parties have come to view most issues as an opportunity to score points with voters, and more issues fall within the purview of central party leaders, whose job is to look out for the electoral interests of the party. In short, parties have allocated increasing resources to devise and disseminate partisan messages about a larger number of issues.

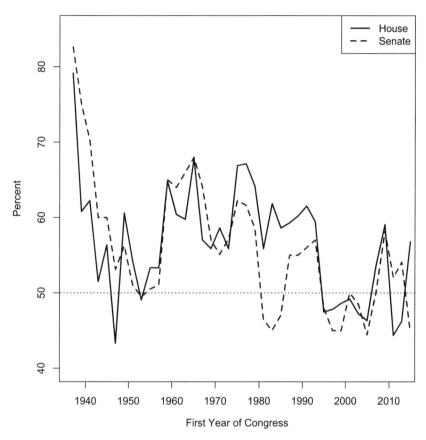

Fig. 1.3. Democratic Party seat share in the House and Senate, 1937–2014. (Compiled by the authors from the official House of Representatives website.)

These activities—a product of the more concerted efforts to gain and retain majority party status—have also encouraged party discipline as an electoral strategy. This happens most conspicuously in policy domains that have the greatest bearing on the parties' reputation with the voting public. Fiscal policy issues, such as spending and taxes, certainly fit into this category, which explains the willingness of congressional Democrats to enact budget process reform when they were losing a public relations battle with President Nixon over spending bills in the early 1970s. But the increased capacity of the parties to engage in public relations efforts and the intensity of the fight for majority control encourages leaders to extend the reach of their party strategies to nearly all issues.

While intense party competition can generate a more party-oriented legislative process, it also can generate tensions within parties over the legislative strategies that they should pursue. These tensions can be particularly pronounced under conditions of divided party control of the House, Senate, and presidency. Two features of federal policy making create strategic challenges for a majority party in one or both houses. The first is the constitutional requirement that the House, Senate, and president approve legislation, at least in the common circumstance that a two-thirds majority in both houses cannot be mustered to override a veto. The second is the ability of a Senate minority to block most legislation by conducting a filibuster. Strategic responses to these challenges range from compromise to intransigence, and everything between.

Well-informed partisans with similar policy goals can differ about how to deal with their party's challenges. It is not always easy to estimate how the other party will respond, how the public will evaluate the party's moves, or how to balance electoral and policy goals. Moreover, uncertainty about near-term control of the House or Senate may increase the importance of making smart strategic moves and therefore exacerbate the tensions among factions within a majority party. On one side, fear of losing majority control may encourage caution in a majority party and some party members may advocate pulling back on the party's agenda to maintain appeal to middle-of-the-road voters. On the other side, anticipation of losing control may motivate some party members to insist that every effort be made to accomplish the party's policy goals while they are still in the majority. Nonetheless, it is important to note that the severity of these tensions are dependent in no small way on the degree of uncertainty that the parties have about gaining or retaining majority party status.

Intense party competition may bleed into the legislative process and affect nearly every aspect of the parties' strategies. In the case of post-passage politics, intense concern about the implications of outcomes on major legislation for the electoral interests of the parties motivates close supervision and even direct control of post-passage negotiations by central party leaders. Party interests, quite simply, dominate committee interests. Committee leaders may be able to protect party interests, and their expertise remains valuable to their parent parties, but the overriding interest in gaining credit or avoiding blame for the party leads rank-and-file members to expect their leaders to be proactive in every stage, including the post-passage stage, of the legislative process.

The traditional committee-oriented decision-making process is not fully compatible with a party-oriented process. Deliberations about policy substance and political strategy move from committee rooms to party caucus meetings and leadership offices. Conference committees, which are a natural extension of committee-oriented decision making in the parent chambers, operate under severe constraints when the parties have strong expectations for outcomes. Conference committees may even become inefficient and unnecessary if key decisions are made by party leaders and can be written into legislation without the use of conference reports.

Partisan Polarization

While the electoral insecurity of the parties may affect choices about process in Congress, another feature of parties is critical to understanding the extent to which the rank-and-file membership is willing to empower party leaders to pursue these strategies—party polarization. The polarization of congressional parties is grounded in the electoral constituencies that elect members of both parties and the policy views of the candidates elected to Congress. The intensity of party competition for control of the House and Senate, and the relative size of the two parties in each chamber, contribute to polarization by encouraging partisan gamesmanship and inspiring disciplined parties. But a large part of the conflict between the parties in Congress is rooted in the different constituencies to which the candidates of the two parties appeal for votes.

Figure 1.4 shows the levels of polarization in both chambers from 1937 to 2014.[6] We observe a striking increase in polarization between the parties beginning in the 1970s. In later chapters, we show that this polarization is motivated by high levels of party voting across numerous policy domains. This growth in party voting has been attributed to the coalescence of party preferences that began in the middle of the twentieth century. However, it was not until the reforms of the 1970s that the parties were able to more fully pursue (and realize) their legislative objectives. As we discuss in more detail below, these reforms expanded the authority of party leaders and enabled them to better control policy outcomes. In turn, these reforms further spurred the growth of polarization.

The conditional party government thesis contends that rising levels of polarization (i.e., increasing interparty heterogeneity and intraparty homogeneity) led members to cede more power to party leaders to pursue partisan ends (Rohde 1991). Given that the difference in utility between policy victories and losses grows with polarization, members vest power in their leaders in the hopes of improving their odds of ending up on the winning side. Moreover, minority party members have greater incentive to

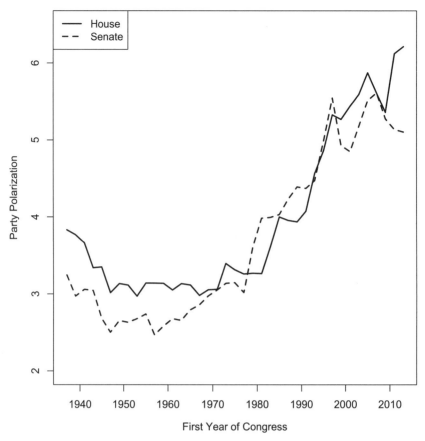

Fig. I.4. Party polarization in the House and Senate, 1937–2014. (Compiled by the authors from voteview.org.)

obstruct majority initiatives in an effort to avoid those policy loses. Since majority party leaders are charged with pursuing the majority's interests in an increasingly uncertain and hostile environment, party leaders are less likely to entrust the legislative process to entities over which they have little control. Put another way, party leaders are more inclined to retain control of the legislative process when policies are important to the party's reputation and their fellow partisans share a common view of the policy goals to be achieved. This was an important motivation for the institutional reforms of the 1970s that sought to centralize legislative authority.

The effects of polarization surely extend to post-passage decision making. At a minimum, partisan polarization is likely to reduce the role of the minority in conference delegations. When the conferees are polarized along party lines, no minority party support for the conference report is needed to gain a numeric majority and therefore minority party conferees are likely to be excluded from the informal deliberations that occur in nearly all conferences. If the House and Senate are controlled by the same party, the minority party may have no meaningful voice in conference at all.

Partisan polarization also undercuts the role of conferences. If negotiations are transferred from committee leaders to party leaders, conference committees serve little purpose. They might ratify agreements negotiated by party leaders in the form of conference reports, but, as we will see, there are more efficient alternatives to conference reports as a way to acquire House and Senate approval of the outcome of leader-motivated negotiations.

Partisan Control of the House, Senate, and Presidency

The challenges associated with intense party competition for control of the policy-making institutions and deep policy differences between the parties depend, at least in part, on whether one party controls the House, Senate, and presidency (Binder and Lee 2016). When one party controls all three institutions, the partisan rhetoric may be sharp but the standard committee-floor-conference process is unlikely to be problematic for the advantaged party. In contrast, since both parties are focused on scoring political points against an opposition that holds dramatically different policy objectives, periods of divided party control of the three institutions can stall legislative productivity. Gridlock entails delay and delay may mean bumping up against deadlines for critical and time-sensitive legislative action, like government funding and lifting the debt limit, that, if it is not passed, causes considerable harm to government and the reputations of elected officials. Impending deadlines on legislation that has important implications for public attitudes about the parties and that nearly everyone agrees must pass in some form, raises the stakes of the legislating and therefore pushes decisions up to the president and congressional party leaders.

The combination of intense partisanship and divided party control, along with the frequent need to negotiate consequential legislation under emergency circumstances, puts the standard legislative process for major bills in jeopardy. Informal discussions among top leaders substitute for negotiations among committee leaders, and the need to avoid procedural obstacles is keen. The desire to minimize the time required to pass compromise legislation leads both party and committee leaders to bring legislation directly to the floor without additional committee or conference consideration. In the period of high partisan polarization, divided government is commonplace. In fact, from 1981 through 2016, there were only four Congresses in which one party controlled the House, Senate, and presidency.

Inherited Institutions: Weakening the Seniority System

Congressional decision-making processes are governed by rules and precedents, but these rules and precedents are determined by House and Senate majorities and can be changed by majorities. Institutional reforms throughout the twentieth century, which came in response to the changing demands on the membership, set the stage for much of the variation we see in the use of conference committees (and other post-passage methods) across time. In particular, reforms in the latter half of the twentieth century incrementally changed long-standing institutions that extended considerable autonomy to standing committees, and standing committee chairs in particular. These reforms, over time, served to shift the power center in Congress away from standing committees and toward the (majority) party leadership. Since conference committees have historically been a means for parent committee members to participate in post-passage decision making, it should come as no surprise that the prominence of conference as a means of resolving intercameral differences is closely related to the relative strength of standing committees across time.

There is little debate that the Congress of the first half of the twentieth century can best be characterized as a committee-dominated one (Deering and Smith 1997). Institutional reforms taking place in the early twentieth century aimed to wrest power away from party leaders and place it firmly in the hands of the standing committees. Committee powers were codified, and party leaders were denied committee leadership positions. As a result, committees had near-dictatorial rights over the legislation referred to them. Perhaps more important during this time, the informal institution (i.e., custom) of the seniority system was adopted in both chambers. While formal rules gave technical control of committee composition to party leaders, the practice of the seniority system imposed near-binding constraints on party leaders. The seniority system ensured that the longest, continuously-serving members of Congress would not only have the ability to select their preferred committee and subcommittee assignments but they would also gain control of committee chairs. Failure by party leaders to comply with the norms of seniority would be met with retribution from the rank-and-file membership—something members in the early twentieth century were more than willing to exercise in response to the excessive use of authority by party leaders (e.g., the 1910 Cannon revolt). In fact, legislative expert George Galloway wrote in 1953 that "in no other place, perhaps, does seniority or length of service carry so much weight as it does in the Congress of the United States" (Galloway 1953, 367). Several other reforms, too numerous to discuss in detail here, also served to further the independence of committees throughout the first half of the twentieth century.[7]

However, by the 1960s and 1970s, issues arose on the agenda that proved to be salient with the voting public, such as civil rights and the environment. Not only were these issues salient, but they were highly contentious, and spurred rapid growth in the interest group community. Therefore, the emergence of these issues placed significant new demands on liberal members to pursue policy change. However, liberal Democrats were stymied by the comparatively smaller conservative faction of their own party, creating turmoil within the party. How is it that conservative Democrats, who were fewer in number than their liberal counterparts, were able to block the liberal agenda? The seniority system had ensured that conservative southern Democrats would disproportionately chair standing committees, by way of the South having a longer history with the Democratic Party. These southern Democratic chairs took advantage of the expansive negative powers granted to standing committee chairs to block liberal proposals in committee. Quite simply, the institutional reforms intended to bolster the powers of standing committees and their chairs now stood between the liberal Democrats and policy change. This intraparty frustration would prompt a series of reforms that have had long-lasting effects on the autonomy of committees.

Perhaps the most noteworthy reforms made to the committee system during this time were the 1970s decisions by Democrats and Republicans in both chambers to weaken the importance of the seniority system in the selection of committee chairs and ranking members. In 1971, House Democrats empowered their Committee on Committees—the committee charged with nominating committee delegations—to recommend committee chairs without strict reliance on seniority, and instituted provisions that allowed the Democratic caucus to challenge committee chairs. These changes to their party rules gave Democrats the opportunity to request a separate vote on any committee chair or member upon the request of 10 members. At the same time, Republicans adopted similar rules changes regarding the selection of ranking members. At the outset of the following Congress (in 1973), House Democrats automated the election of committee chairs by requiring that the caucus vote on all committee chairs and not just those who were the target of a request for a vote, and permitted a secret vote on the chairs with the request of 20 percent of the caucus. The Senate parties, likewise, reformed their party rules during this period to make committee leaders subject to party support.[8] The party reforms gave members who were unhappy with the behavior of committee chairs/ranking members from their own party an opportunity to circumvent the seniority system and elect committee leaders who were friendlier to their cause.

It was not long before members took advantage of these rules changes. In 1975, House Democrats voted to unseat three senior committee chairs. Each of the unseated chairs was a conservative southern Democrat, who held policy preferences that were out of step with the rest of the caucus. These unseated chairs were subsequently replaced by liberal Northern Democrats. Six other committee chairs voluntarily abdicated their seats, which may have mitigated the number of chairs ousted by the caucus. Crook and Hibbing (1985) find evidence that these reforms almost instantaneously increased the party loyalty of senior members. Having lost their powerful committee seats, and seeing that committees were increasingly subject to the party caucus, southern Democrats began to retire or switch parties to the more ideologically congruent Republican Party (Rohde 1991; Yoshinaka 2016). Naturally, with the decline in southern Democrats, this led to increasing intraparty homogeneity and interparty heterogeneity, which we have already argued is an important factor in post-passage decision making. Nevertheless, with committee chairs having to answer to the party caucus, they no longer enjoyed the independence they once did, as power shifted away from standing committees and was placed in the hands of party leaders.

Inherited Institutions: Reforming the Budget Process

Nearly simultaneously with the committee reforms that weakened the seniority system, the House created a new budget process in 1974 that would both shift power away from standing committees toward party leaders and reduce the number of measures that could be considered in conference. Before the 1974 reform, Congress did not act on any piece of legislation that defined the overall budget of spending, revenue, and deficits/surpluses for the federal government. The president submitted a budget, but Congress only acted on separate appropriations and revenue bills. In the early 1970s, interest in budget reform was spurred by chronic deficits and political tensions between the Democratic Congress and Republican president Nixon. In retrospect, the deficits of that period seem small, but they were unprecedented for a time without a declared war. The shortfall was largely the result of new and expensive domestic initiatives (e.g., President Lyndon Johnson's Great Society program) and the Vietnam War. Promising to gain control of the budget, Nixon won the 1968 presidential election and then proceeded to engage in intense battles with the Democratic Congress over spending and taxes. These battles motivated Congress to strengthen its own budget-making capacities by adopting the Budget Act.[9]

The Budget Act created a process for coordinating the actions of the appropriations, authorizing, and tax committees. Each May, Congress would pass a preliminary budget resolution setting nonbinding targets for expenditures and revenues. During the summer, Congress would pass the individual bills authorizing and appropriating funds for federal programs, as well as any new tax legislation. Then, in September, Congress would adopt a second budget resolution, providing final spending ceilings. This resolution might require adjustments to some of the decisions made during the summer months. Those adjustments would be reflected in the second resolution, and additional legislation, written by the proper committees, would then be drafted to make the necessary changes. This process of adjustment was labeled "reconciliation," to reflect the need to reconcile the earlier decisions with the second budget resolution. The reconciliation legislation was to be enacted by October 1, the first day of the federal government's fiscal year.

The Budget Act provided for two new committees, the House and Senate Budget Committees. The budget committees write the budget resolutions and package reconciliation legislation from various committees ordered to adjust the programs under their jurisdiction.

The Budget Act also modified Senate floor procedures in a critical way. The act barred nongermane amendments and set a limit of 20 hours on debate over budget resolutions and reconciliation legislation. These rules mean that budget measures cannot be loaded with extraneous floor amendments or killed by a Senate filibuster. However, the rules did not restrict the kinds of provisions committees could write into budget measures. Consequently, the door was left open for committees to include provisions unrelated to spending and taxes in reconciliation bills. This became a common practice once reconciliation bills became a central feature of the budget-making process in the 1980s. The "Byrd rule," named after Senator Robert C. Byrd (D-WV), was adopted in the 1980s to limit the provisions of reconciliation bills to budget-related matters.

Starting in 1980, reconciliation bills, which must be authorized by a budget resolution, began to be considered before the traditional appropriations, authorization, and tax legislation was passed. This allowed for more rapid action on a final package of deficit reduction provisions, although the term "reconciliation" became somewhat inappropriate. Because they are protected by limits on debate and amendments, reconciliation bills have been an important legislative vehicle for efforts to enact spending cuts and pass tax legislation since then. In fact, budget procedures have altered the strategies of legislators pursuing spending and tax policy goals. Appropriations bills became governed by spending caps set in budget resolutions. Policy proposals that once were considered as stand-alone bills could sometimes be packaged in reconciliation bills.

The 1974 budget process was intended to give more emphasis to the aggregate effects of spending and tax decisions, and more explicitly link spending and tax decisions to an overall budget. It has worked out that way, and with important consequences. Aggregate budget decisions focused attention on the size and role of government, which emerged as the central difference between the parties. Spending and tax decisions that once drew little attention from most legislators and party leaders now were connected to larger budget issues that divided the parties. Once decentralized, committee-by-committee, bill-by-bill legislating was replaced by legislating concentrated in a few bills, constructed by the budget committees in some cases, and always supervised by top party leaders.

Just as the budget process was intended to reduce the influence of the separate standing committees over fiscal policy, the budget process concentrated important bits and pieces of policy into fewer bills. In turn, much important legislation is diverted to fewer budget, spending, and tax measures, and with less legislation being managed in the traditional way by the senior members of the major standing committees. Another important implication of this reform is that the number of conference committees required to negotiate over the differences in House- and Senate-passed legislation was bound to fall. In short, a number of individual fiscal measures, which at one time were separately considered in conference, were now being lumped together.

Inherited Institutions: Other Noteworthy Reforms

In addition to the reforms to the seniority system and the budget process, other reforms from the 1970s forward sought to make committees more accountable to rank-and-file members and party leaders. While too numerous and involved to offer a comprehensive handling of them here, a few developments in formal rules deserve attention for their implications for post-passage decision making:

- sunshine rules;
- increasing bill referral options for the Speaker;
- voting rules changes;
- new conference committee rules; and
- changes in the allocation of rank-and-file resources.

Sunshine rules, which refer to the collection of rules that require committees to open their practices to the public, meant that committees could no longer operate exclusively behind closed doors and out of the public (and their colleagues') eye. Among other mandates, the sunshine rules required that roll-call votes taken in committee be published in open records, and markups be held in public session unless a majority of committee members vote to close the meeting. Conference committees are subject to many of the same requirements. The goal of these rules was to open committee practices to scrutiny from both outside and inside the chambers. As a result, sunshine rules provide rank-and-file members, and party leaders in particular, with a greater ability to monitor the behavior of standing committees, thus reducing the capacity of standing committees to act without constraint.

In 1974, reforms to bill referral practices fundamentally changed the amount of discretion that the Speaker has in determining which committee(s) will have legislative authority over a particular measure. Prior to this time, the Speaker was required to refer legislation to the single committee with the most relevant jurisdiction, which, in turn, gave that committee near-monopoly control over the legislation (and all legislation in its jurisdiction). Following a 1974 rules change, however, the Speaker was given the authority to send legislation to multiple committees, either jointly, sequentially, or in parts.[10] The Senate is, likewise, able to refer legislation to multiple committees, although the practice is far less common than in the House. The power to make multiple referrals significantly enhanced the ability of party leaders to control the legislative process. Leaders were afforded the ability to make strategic considerations regarding which committees will have access to revise which portions of the legislation and in what order.

The 1970s also saw the adoption of electronic voting in the House. While on the surface this may seem to be wholly unrelated to commit-

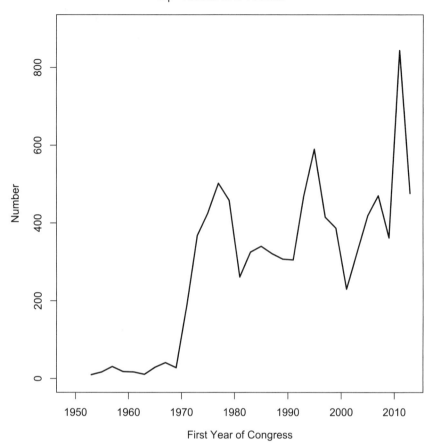

Fig. 1.5. Number of floor amendments subject to a roll-call vote in the House, 1953–2014. (Compiled by the authors from Political Institutions and Public Choice Roll-Call Database.)

tee autonomy, the introduction of electronic voting dramatically altered the mix of votes considered on the floor. In particular, electronic voting led to a marked rise in House floor amending activity, as shown in figure 1.5. Whereas recorded votes were prohibitively time-consuming prior to the advent of electronic voting, they could now be carried out in mere moments. As a result, recorded votes on amendments motivated members to challenge the decisions made in committee, given the public availability of information regarding their voting behavior and the ease of doing so.

Additional House rules changes in the 1970s also challenged the norm that gave senior standing committee members effectively unfettered access to conference committees. This practice meant that the Speaker had little authority over conferences, since appointments to conference were more or less routinized. This would change in 1975 and again in 1977 with the passage of House rules that instructed the Speaker to appoint conference delegations that are representative of the chamber's position on the policy, and to appoint members to conference who sponsored major provisions of the legislation, respectively. In the aftermath of these rules changes, Speakers were less willing to simply accept the slates proposed by committee chairs (Smith 1989). A 1993 House rules change further strengthened the appointment powers of the Speaker by giving the Speaker the authority to remove a member from conference at any time, even after the conference has begun. Taken together, these rules changes reduce the reliance of the Speaker on committee chair recommendations, and empower the Speaker to reward members who are supportive of party positions (Maltzman 1997).

Changes in the allocation of resources across time have also resulted in a reduction in the resource disparity between committees and rank-and-file members. Rules changes have allowed members to acquire a more expansive personal staff than earlier periods in congressional history. In addition, there is now a larger network of support agencies (e.g., the Congressional Research Service) to which members can turn for information. As a result, the advantages that committees have over rank-and-file members are a fraction of what they once were. Therefore, there is less incentive for members to defer to committees on the basis of superior policy information and expertise than there was in earlier periods marked by greater resource inequality.

While institutions in the first half of the twentieth century served to enhance committee autonomy, reforms of the latter half of the century reversed this trend. Since conference committees are an extension of the committee system, these shifts in power between committees and party leaders (which now clearly advantage party leaders) should have important implications for the use of conference. We argue that the institutional changes documented above, while certainly related to other factors that affect the use of conference, nonetheless change the capacity of members and party leaders to pursue their goals. That is, while these institutional reforms may not alone be responsible for observed changes in post-passage practices, they set the stage for party leaders to seize control when there is sufficient demand for them to do so. Partisan competition and polarization, we argue, drive variation in the demand from rank-and-file members for party leaders to claim a central role in forging policy outcomes.

Contextual Factors

We suggest that partisan competition, partisan polarization, and inherited institutions are the chief determinants of changes in the use of post-passage resolution mechanisms. These factors represent important structural changes in the institutions and composition of the chambers across time. Yet even when we have (relative) stability in these features within a given two-year Congress, we still observe variability in the use of conferences and other post-passage mechanisms. Other, more proximate, bill-by-bill factors surely influence post-passage decision making. We propose that these contextual factors include (1) the importance of a measure to the majority's collective reputation, (2) the information needs of the chambers with respect to a measure, and (3) the time constraints surrounding the consideration of a particular measure.

To be sure, the effects of these contextual factors are influenced by the macro-level ones discussed above. For instance, we know that an increasing number of issues become important to a party's reputation, and the consequences of policy losses are more dire, when polarization rises. Therefore, on average, we would expect to see a greater preponderance of measures that are important to the parties in Congresses with high levels of polarization. Nevertheless, these contextual factors should be viewed as individual-level, and secondary, considerations made by party leaders when the macro-level factors are stable across post-passage cases.

Consistent with our discussion above, we start from the assumption that party leaders will be less likely to delegate important stages of the legislative process to decentralized units when the consequences of policy losses are nontrivial. If a measure is of particular importance to the majority party's reputation, then we would naturally conclude that party leaders will wish to retain more control over the process. After all, managing a party's reputation (i.e., brand name) is one of the most important responsibilities of party leaders (Cox and McCubbins 2005, 2007).

However, party leaders, from time to time, are willing to cede legislative authority, even on important measures, as an exchange for some other provision. Vander Wielen (2012) contends that conferences possess informational advantages that reduce the risk of bargaining failure, which is more likely to occur in the exchange of amendments. Therefore, party leaders are willing to make some policy sacrifices to capitalize on the informational advantages held by conference committees. In a similar vein, Krehbiel (1991) argues that party leaders extend decision-making protections to committees and conferences in order to reap informational gains.

A final contextual consideration is *when* in the two-year Congress a particular measure is being considered. All measures that fail passage within the two-year period, regardless of what stage they are at in the legislative process, are deemed dead, and must be reintroduced in the following Congress. This is a particularly troubling prospect for measures at advanced stages of the legislative process, such as the post-passage stage, for which members have likely invested considerable amounts of time and resources already. Under these circumstances, party leaders may prefer efficient post-passage mechanisms even if they produce some opportunity for policy slack. Conference committees provide an efficient alternative of this variety.

Conclusion

We have witnessed a dramatic change in post-passage politics since the middle of the twentieth century. Whereas conference committees were once a common means of resolving legislative differences between the House and Senate, they have now all but disappeared. We theorize that the near demise of the conference committee in recent years reflects the mutually reinforcing effects of three overarching factors—party competition, party polarization, and inherited institutions. The interconnectedness of these factors has been well established by other scholars. Suffice it to say that changes in these factors are intricately intertwined and have important implications for the locus of power in Congress. We theorize that observed changes in these factors in recent decades have created powerful incentives for members to vest greater authority over post-passage decision making in the central party leadership. Consequently, party leaders have claimed a more pivotal role in resolving intercameral differences, and post-passage mechanisms that extend comparatively more independence to the rank-and-file membership, like conference committees, have subsequently been marginalized.

Intense competition for majority control of the House and Senate over several decades has encouraged parties to more aggressively pursue partisan messaging on a larger number of issues, which has contributed to the increasing polarization of the parties. In turn, the sharp policy differences between the parties have heightened the perceived importance of election outcomes. With rising partisan conflict, congressional majorities have incrementally changed institutions to further empower the party caucus, and party leaders in particular. Regardless of the temporal ordering of these changes, the important point is that they have uniformly led to an environment in which the consequences associated with legislative battles are significant. In the case of the House, where a cohesive majority can impose its agenda and pass its legislation, this has meant more exclusion of the minority from meaningful participation in policy making—in committee, on the floor, and in conference. In the Senate, where a large minority can obstruct action by the majority, this has meant more filibustering and more gridlock.

These developments have direct implications for post-passage politics, which we detail in the following chapters. As we will see, post-passage processes have gone through two waves of changes—one in the 1970s and another starting in the 1990s—that changed the frequency with which bills went to conference and the structure of conference committees. In chapter 2, we outline how the use of conferences committees and other mechanisms for resolving House-Senate differences have changed over the last half century. In chapter 3, we consider the implications of these changes for the partisan bias of conference committees. In chapter 4, we dig deeper into the legislation most deeply affected by these changes and illustrate the systematic variation across policies and committees that remains, even in recent Congresses, and serves to qualify the general patterns that are our primary focus.

TWO

Two Waves of Change
in Post-Passage Methods

On Christmas Eve, 2009, the Senate passed its version of the Affordable Care Act, also known as Obamacare, by a 60–39 vote with no Republican support. The 60-vote coalition was precisely the minimum required to invoke cloture the day before and get a vote on the bill. Senator Edward Kennedy (D-MA) had died in August and was temporarily replaced by a Democrat, retaining the 60 votes for the bill. The House had passed the bill 220–215 in early November, also with no Republican votes and 39 Democrats voting against the bill. The next step would be to resolve the differences between the very long House and Senate versions of the bill—the House version was 1,990 pages long, or about 230,000 words.[1]

Before the House and Senate could approve a compromise version, Senator Scott Brown (R-MA), a Republican, was narrowly elected to replace Kennedy for the rest of his term. This meant that there were only 59 votes for cloture on a compromise version, in the form of either a conference report or a clean bill, so the Democrats devised a new plan. They had the House pass the Senate version and then both houses passed a separate bill, which they labeled a reconciliation bill, to change the terms of the bill they had just enacted to reflect compromises between the two versions. The rules governing the reconciliation process, found in the Budget Act, prevent a Senate filibuster by limiting debate and allowed a simple majority to approve the compromises.

The events of 2009–10 were truly remarkable. One of the most important acts of Congress in recent decades was in final form as a result of the close supervision of top party leaders and an ad hoc, unconventional means of resolving House-Senate differences. In this case, the House adopted the Senate bill on the condition that a second bill would be passed immediately to amend the first bill and the second bill would be a budget reconciliation bill that prevented minority obstruction in the Senate.

These procedural moves were sharply criticized by Republicans. Of course, Republicans had used reconciliation procedures in new ways to pass tax bills a few years earlier. Indeed, few people who were paying close attention to the ways majority party leaders were adapting parliamentary processes to evolving political circumstances were surprised by the Democrats' inventiveness in 2010.

The evolving mechanisms of House-Senate reconciliation, and the degree that they are required, are a product of the larger changes in how the House and Senate make policy. In this chapter, we elaborate on that theme by describing and explaining the historical pattern in the methods used to resolve House-Senate differences since the 1960s. We characterize the pattern for three different periods:

- Pre-1970s: mid-twentieth century dominance of conference committees;
- 1970s-1990s: a transition to fewer but larger bills, larger conferences, and the use of multi-committee conferences;
- Post-1990s: the gradual demise of conference committees as the primary means for resolving House-Senate differences on major legislation.

There are other important details, particularly in the House, but these three periods provide a convenient way to think about the manner in which the House and Senate responded to evolving political forces that motivated important changes in how the final versions of bills were crafted.

Broad Patterns in Making Law

The House and Senate must approve legislation in identical form before it is sent to the president, but the Constitution gives little guidance as to how the bodies should go about resolving House-Senate differences. Rather, the House and Senate create their own methods by adopting rules and precedents. They can even set aside their standing rules on a case-by-case basis to fashion legislation that can gain the approval of both chambers.

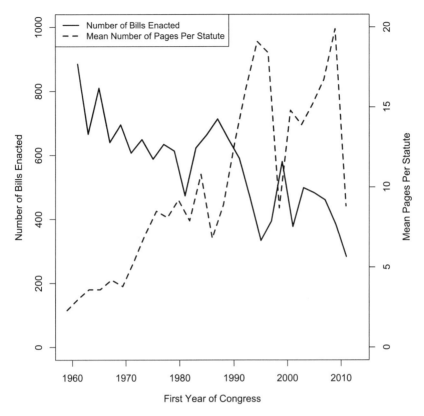

Fig. 2.1. Number of and pages in enacted bills, 1961–2012. (Compiled by the authors from *Vital Statistics on Congress* [chapter 6].)

The structure of the bills passing the House and Senate changed in an important way over the last half century. The overall number of separate bills and joint resolutions enacted into public law declined while the average size of the legislative measures enacted increased (figure 2.1). This pattern reflects several trends in congressional policy making that we address in the next section. As we will see, post-passage politics contributed to this trend, particularly in recent years, but most of the decline in the number of bills passed and the corresponding increase in the pages per bill passed has little to do with post-passage dynamics. As fewer but larger bills were constructed by the House and Senate, the number of bills sent to conference or that involved a complex exchange of amendments between the houses declined. Instead, there was a proportionate rise in more streamlined methods for resolving House-Senate differences.

To see these trends in sharper detail, let's first revisit the basic paths for getting a House- or Senate-passed bill through Congress. There are five such paths:

1. *Simple passage.* One chamber passes the bill and the other chamber passes the same bill without any amendments.
2. *One-step exchange of amendments.* One chamber passes the bill, the other chamber passes it with one or more amendments, and the first-acting chamber agrees to the other chamber's amendments.
3. *Two (or-more)-step exchange of amendments.* The chambers send the bill back and forth as each chamber amends the other chamber's amendments; the process ends when the bill and all amendments, as amended, are approved by both houses.
4. *Conference committee.* The two chambers agree to a conference and the conference report is approved in both houses.
5. *Combination of conference and exchange of amendments.* Two possibilities exist in this path: a conference committee report is approved with an exchange of amendments on matters in disagreement (common); or an exchange of amendments is followed by a conference committee (rare).

The five paths can be grouped into two categories, simple and complex processes. The first two paths, simple passage and a one-step exchange of amendments, usually involve simple bills with few interchamber differences and are labeled "Simple" in figure 2.2. The other paths involve conferences or multistage exchanges of amendments and usually engage legislators in more involved negotiations. They are labeled "Complex" in figure 2.2.

The mix of paths taken to enactment changed greatly after the 1970s. As the bills enacted became fewer but larger, the number and percentage of bills going to conference or subject to multistep exchanges of amendments declined. At the same time, the percentage of all enacted bills that did not go to conference or require a multistep exchange of amendments steadily increased.

The First Wave

Figure 2.2 exposes the changes in general patterns of post-passage politics that we highlight in this chapter. The mid-twentieth century pattern of an

Number

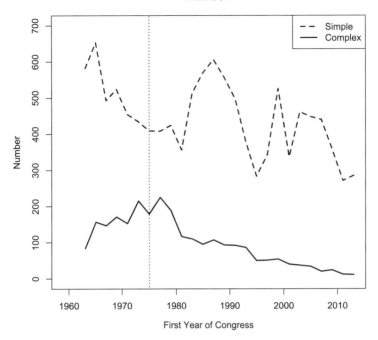

Percent

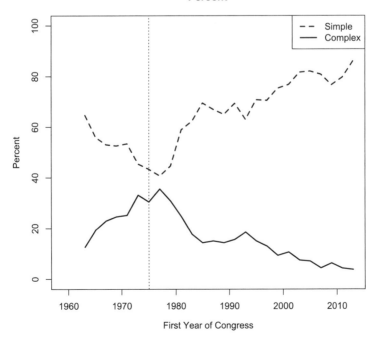

Fig. 2.2. Number and percentage of public laws, by simple and complex reconciliation processes, 1963–2014. (Compiled by the authors from *CQ Almanac*.)

increasing number of conference committees as the congressional agenda expanded was reversed in the 1970s. This turning point, which we refer to as the first wave of change, reflected the changes in the committee system and budget process that ultimately diminished reliance on conferences. This was accompanied by greater participation in individual conferences and a corresponding increase in the size of conference delegations, particularly for the House. We later discuss the second wave of change in post-passage methods taking place in the mid-1990s that further reinforced this downward trend in the number of public laws that were approved by a conference committee or subject to a multistep exchange of amendments.

The reversal in the patterns of conference use in the 1970s may, at first, appear puzzling. Bills became larger and more complex and yet the number and proportion of enacted bills treated in conference or a complex exchange of amendments dwindled. As we argue below, the reason is plain: as partisan battles intensified, formal committee-based processes for resolving House-Senate differences were often replaced with informal party-based negotiations. Conferences and negotiations among committee leaders were supplanted by negotiations among party leaders and presidents who structure large package deals and then arrange for final House and Senate action, often without conferences. Following the first wave of change, bills ballooned in size and the "regular" process of committee-led policy making was set aside in favor of summit-level bargaining by top party leaders and the president.

Factionalism among House Democrats

In chapter 1, we outlined how interparty competition, the distribution of policy preferences, and institutional rules influence the kind of post-passage politics that emerge in Congress. We see these principles at work in the 1970s, during which there were fundamental changes in the process of resolving House-Senate differences. These changes were driven by reforms advocated by liberal Democrats in the House, who were seeking to reduce the power of the conservative chairs of standing committees and assert the power of the liberal majority within the party.

Democrats enjoyed House and Senate majorities in all but two Congresses between 1933 and 1980, and their practices and internal dynamics shaped post-passage politics in important ways. During most of this period, Democrats were a diverse party that enjoyed sufficiently large majorities in most Congresses that there was little need for concern about losing majority party status. In this context, strong central party leadership was unessential, and committee members were happy to take the lead in writing legislation.

During this period, many of the Democratic committee chairs ran their committee activities in an autocratic fashion. They determined whether their committees would have subcommittees, appointed subcommittees and their chairs, determined whether legislation would be marked up in committee or subcommittee, managed important bills on the floor, and controlled the appointment of staff. They also determined who would represent the committee in conference committee delegations by making recommendations to the Speaker, who, with few exceptions, would follow their advice. In nearly all cases, they listed themselves and led negotiations with their counterpart in the other chamber. In this way, full committee chairs dominated every stage of the regular legislative process, including conference committees, which were a de facto bargaining forum for the leaders of the House and Senate committees where legislation originated.

This committee-oriented system dominated by senior committee members disproportionately benefited conservative Democrats. Southern and conservative Democrats were more routinely reelected, and thereby acquired the committee seniority necessary to become committee chairs. This was obvious to liberal Democrats in the 1950s, but it became a matter of serious objections and reform efforts in the late 1960s.

With Democratic control of Congress seldom in serious jeopardy during the late 1950s through the 1970s, fights over policy often involved a fight for control between conservative and liberal Democrats. The number of liberal Democrats increased during the late 1950s and 1960s, which shifted the balance of power to the liberal faction of the majority party Democrats. As liberals sought to reduce the influence of conservatives over the legislative process, they democratized procedures to allow more of them to become involved at key stages of the legislative process. The democratization process included putting committee chairs up for election in the party caucus, forcing the creation of subcommittees, and sharing power over the internal operations of standing committees with other majority party members by making chairs accountable to the wishes of fellow partisans in the caucus and in committee.

Liberal Democrats also recognized another source of power for committee chairs—the control of conference committee delegations. Conference committee negotiators could determine important legislative outcomes. Even when liberals in committee or on the floor could gain majority support for liberal provisions in a bill, a conservative committee chair opposed to the provisions would likely have access to revise the bill if it went to conference. The traditional pattern of allowing chairs to name a handful of the most senior committee members to a conference gave very few legislators a voice at the conference stage and gave some conservative chairs considerable leeway in working on the final details of legislation in conference. With the general rule being that the House and Senate must accept or reject the conference report as a whole, all that the conferees had to do was make the conference report minimally acceptable to a majority in each chamber. This left most of the details of legislation to the few conferees.

For these reasons, it was natural for liberal reformers to be concerned about conference committee appointments and procedures. With respect to conference appointments, House reformers successfully pushed for the adoption of two rules. A 1975 House rule stipulates that "in appointing members to conference committees the Speaker shall appoint no less than a majority of members who generally supported the House position as determined by the Speaker." The 1975 rule was strengthened in 1977, Thomas "Tip" O'Neill's (D-MA) first year as Speaker, with the additional requirement that "the Speaker shall name members who are primarily responsible for the legislation and shall, to the fullest extent feasible, include the principal proponents of the major provisions of the bill as it passed the House." The initiative for naming conferees continued to reside with the chair of the committee originating a bill, but the new rules signaled that the Speaker would be expected to take a more active role in overseeing conference appointments.

During the same period, two additional noteworthy procedural changes were made. In 1972, the House adopted a rule that created a means to challenge nongermane components of legislation adopted by the Senate or reported by a conference. Previously, the House was required to accept nongermane portions of conference reports or reject the entire bill. Nongermane provisions gave House conferees a means to address or accept legislative language on subjects that were not a part of the original House-passed bill. Under the new rule, a point of order could, and still can, be made that a provision violates the House germaneness rule, which creates an opportunity to vote on the provision in question and thereby challenge the conferees' recommendation. At a minimum, the change forced conferees to be more sensitive to the will of the House majority when considering approaches to compromising with the Senate.

In many cases, the germaneness point of order is waived as a part of a special rule governing floor consideration of a conference report or Senate bill. However, a special rule must receive majority support from the

Rules Committee and on the House floor, and so waiving points of order usually requires the backing of the Speaker and most majority party members. Consequently, abuses of committee discretion in conference can be checked by majority party legislators more readily than before the 1972 rule was adopted.

A second change of significance is the 1974 rule, adopted in both houses, that requires conference meetings to be open to the public unless the conferees of at least one house vote in open session to close the meeting for that day. In practice, informal negotiations take place out of public view, although formal votes usually take place in public session.

The reforms made to the House and Democratic caucus rules led to broadened participation in the conference committees. Expectations changed. The involvement of subcommittees in the consideration of most bills added a set of legislators who expected a role in conference committees. Rank-and-file members insisted on appointment to conferences, and committee chairs, clearly under pressure from their rank-and-file colleagues, forwarded larger conference delegations. The speaker, particularly Speaker O'Neill, was responsive to the demands. In some cases, as we will see, this made conference delegations considerably larger than they were in the past and encouraged creative ways to structure participation in conference.

Efforts to Integrate Policy Making

In the early 1970s, legislators and outside observers, mostly liberals, were concerned about the ability of Congress to address complex issues with its decentralized committee system. In the House, new procedures were invented to create ad hoc committees and to permit a bill to be considered by more than one committee. In the case of multi-committee bills, an implication was that more than one committee had claims to representation on conference delegations and, in some cases, committees demanded exclusive conference jurisdiction over provisions of the legislation referred to their committee. This produced large conference delegations and new ways of structuring conference participation.

Two sets of reforms set the stage for the involvement of multiple committees on a single bill. The first was the advent of multiple referral in the House. Until 1974, the House rule governing the referral of legislation to committee required that the Speaker refer a bill to the committee with predominant jurisdiction over the content of legislation. This created struggles between committees for referral from time to time that would be settled on the basis of accumulated precedents, or would end up with the speaker resolving the issue by choosing among fellow partisans. By the 1970s, legislators also were concerned that many bills that sought to address complex problems would touch on the jurisdictions of several committees, and so a new way was required to consider such bills. Committee jurisdictions could be rearranged to fit new issues, of course, but that might prove to be a never-ending process and still leave many bills straddling committee jurisdictions.

The 1974 rule allowed the Speaker to refer legislation to more than one committee (Davidson, Oleszek, and Kephart 1988; Davidson 1989; Young and Cooper 1993). Over 10 percent of legislation introduced was referred to multiple committees in the 95th and 96th Congresses (1977–1978, 1979–1980), and that percentage rose steadily in subsequent years (King 1997). When multiply referred measures passed the House and Senate and moved to conference, the Speaker, in discussions with committee chairs and others, would have to find a way to satisfy demands for wider representation on conferences. On occasion, the speaker would also have to deal with committee claims for the right to be the exclusive negotiators for certain parts of the legislation. This motivated the creation of subconferences—subgroups of legislators who are assigned responsibility for specified titles, sections, or even paragraphs in legislation.

In retrospect, the second set of reforms, the creation of a new budget process in 1974, was even more important for the future of post-passage decision making. As we noted in chapter 1, budget process reform was a reaction to the Democratic Congress's conflict with Republican president Richard Nixon over spending and the difficulty it faced with enacting a coherent budget of its own. For decades, Congress had enacted a dozen or more appropriations bills, several revenue bills, and many other measures that created obligations for federal programs to spend money; this was done without considering and approving an overall budget. Under the new process, a budget resolution could order multiple committees to report legislation to reduce deficits that would be packaged into a reconciliation bill by the newly created budget committees in the House and Senate.

When the first reconciliation bill was passed in 1980, it represented a significant opportunity for legislators to package legislation into one large bill that might not get far in the process if they were considered as stand-alone measures. A variety of rules and precedents have been adopted since 1980 to limit the content of reconciliation bills to budget-related provisions. Even with these constraints, a wide range of content, organized into titles associated with the recommendations of committees, is packaged in reconciliation bills.

Between 1980 and 2016, 24 reconciliation bills were passed by both houses, and, with the exception of the bills considered in 1983, 2010, and 2016, the bills went to conference. As we describe in greater detail in chapter 4, most of these conference delegations were very large and organized into subconferences, each associated with a title of the bill. The size of these conference delegations reflected the appointment of members from, in some cases, more than a dozen committees in each house. Budget committee members served as conferees for all titles, so we refer to them as "general-purpose conferees" here. Members of the committee responsible for one of the titles usually served as a voting conferee for only one title, and so we label them "limited-purpose conferees" here.

The invention of complex conferences for reconciliation and multiply referred bills eventually produced two types of limited-purpose conferees.[2] When one chamber (more commonly the House) authorizes some conferees to negotiate only on specified matters, it may treat them as "additional" conferees to negotiate along with the general-purpose conferees, which implies that the general-purpose conferees and limited-purpose conferees are combined to determine the outcome for those specified matters. Alternatively, the house with limited-purpose conferees may be the "sole" conferees on specified matters. Both kinds of limited-purpose conferees may be appointed to a conference, subconferences may have overlapping memberships, and, at times, a single member has been appointed for a limited purpose.

The introduction of limited-purpose conferees created some challenges for synchronizing House and Senate expectations about the way conferees approve a conference report (Beth and Rybicki 2003). Both houses operate under precedents that require that a valid conference report must be signed by a majority of conferees from each house, but they differ in how limited-purpose conferees are to be counted in meeting that requirement. The Senate considers a conference report to be valid only when signed by a majority of conferees from each chamber without regard to their status as general- or limited-purpose conferees. This precedent applies even when the Senate has appointed some conferees for a limited purpose. The House considers a report to be valid when signed by a majority of conferees who were appointed to consider each provision, as provided in the order appointing them.

These differences in standards can create confusion. The Senate practice produces a single number for a majority of conferees from each house, while the House practice can produce majority thresholds that vary across the subconferences. In principle, a report that is valid in one house can be invalid in the other. This seldom happens, but, when it becomes a potential problem, the speaker can easily appoint more conferees to synchronize majorities for the two houses (Beth and Rybicki 2003).

The Democrats' Way

From the early 1980s through the early 1990s, most of the committee and budget process reforms that were instituted in the 1970s remained in place, and so did the corresponding practices for structuring and appointing conference committees. All three Democratic speakers during the period—Tip O'Neill (D-MA), James Wright (D-TX), and Thomas Foley (D-WA)—followed a pattern of being inclusive when designing bill referral and conferences. Subconferences were used frequently, and, for nearly every multiple-committee bill, conference negotiations were run by members from the committee originating each part of the bill.

In contrast, the Senate never experienced dramatic changes in how it handled bill referral or conferences. Whether under Democratic or Republican control, the Senate never embraced the use of subconferences like their House counterparts. The Senate's tendency to avoid subconferences reflects, at least in part, its precedent of counting a majority of conference report signatories from the full number of conferees. This puts a premium on the overall balance of views among Senate conferees and reduces the value of a subconference structure. Nevertheless, on very large omnibus bills, the Senate has made use of limited-purpose conferences.

The 1992 energy bill conference was handled in a manner typical for large, complicated legislation during the post-reform, Democratic era. The bill was referred to 10 House committees and included sections from most of them. The Senate bill originated in one committee but touched on the jurisdictions of many more. The eventual conference had 102 House conferees and 32 Senate conferees. As *Congressional Quarterly* reported as the conference committee convened for the first time, "most of the real negotiating is expected to take place in dozens of staff meetings and phone calls over the next several weeks" (Idelson 1992, 2710). The bill was cited by many Democrats as having taken the practice of multiple referral and appointing large conferences too far. Legislators complained that these practices resulted in excessive delays that plagued various stages of the legislation's consideration.

The most serious complaints about post-passage methods during the 1980s and early 1990s came from minority party members (Oleszek 2008). While conferences continued to be used for most important legislation, formal conference meetings involved little deliberation and give-and-take among conferees. Instead, committee leaders and top staff tended toward negotiating details in private meetings and then bringing their handiwork to conference meetings for ratification. This process reflected the difficulty of resolving differences among Democrats, but it also reflected the judgment of Democrats that Republicans had such different views that including them in discussions would serve no meaningful purpose since most Republicans were expected to oppose whatever legislation emerged from conference.

The Second Wave

The second wave of change occurred after Republicans won new House and Senate majorities in the 1994 elections, the first midterm election of the Democratic Clinton administration. The period to follow would be marked by historically high levels of partisan polarization and persistently intense battles for control of Congress. Step-by-step, the parties built larger campaign and communications teams and leaders gave more and more attention to winning seats in the next election. The character of the legislative process changed in both houses, with important implications for the ways that the House and Senate resolved their differences.

The House

On the House side, a series of developments in the committee system had implications for post-passage decision-making processes. The new Republican Speaker, Newt Gingrich (R-GA), began the era by following through on promises to change the way the House conducted its business. He insisted on exercising firm control over the selection of committee chairs, committee assignments, the flow of legislation from committee to the floor, and the appointment of conferences. With the backing of his party, Gingrich emphasized discipline and efficiency. He expected committees to meet deadlines for reporting major legislation and expected his fellow partisans to support the party program.

Gingrich reduced the size of House committees, cut committee staff budgets, and enlarged leadership staff. The Republican committee chairs were not bound by the Democrats' rules to use subcommittees and most of the chairs returned to strong centralized control of their committees' decision-making processes. Moreover, the Republicans changed the House rule on multiple referral of legislation to require that the Speaker designate a primary committee, which meant that one committee and its chair would take the lead on the floor and in post-passage action.

These changes stemmed from the Republicans' more hierarchical view of the House—chairs should control their committees and the party and its leader should control the chairs (Aldrich and Rohde 2009). When a committee chair did not share the leadership's views about an important bill, Gingrich had the bill written by a task force or staff, and then brought to the floor without a markup by the committee with formal jurisdiction. Gingrich's successor, Dennis Hastert (R-IL), vowed to loosen the reins on committees, but the process remained far more party-oriented and much less committee-oriented.

These developments promised to reduce the size and simplify the structure of conference delegations, and to increase the involvement of central party leaders in intercameral negotiations. Given that majority party conferees were expected to toe the party line and consult with the party leadership on key issues, large conference delegations were of little utility (and perhaps even disadvantageous to party leaders).

The Senate

The new Senate majority leader, Bob Dole (R-KS), and his successor, Trent Lott (R-MS), could not run the Senate in the same way that Gingrich and Hastert ran the House, but Senate Republicans were benefiting from greater cohesiveness, too, and senators were equally concerned about the party's electoral prospects. As in the House, the size of party staffs dedicated to campaigns and public relations grew. With majority control of both houses in doubt, it was a period of intensifying partisan competition.

Further complicating post-passage processes was growing minority obstructionism in the Senate (Smith 2014). Filibusters were rare in the Senate before the 1970s, and became a regular feature of legislating in the Senate in the 1970s and 1980s. Still, the number of filibusters and cloture votes remained about a half dozen per year during those two decades (figure 2.3). That changed in the 1990s. Counting filibusters is not easy, but the frequency of obstructive efforts at least doubled between the 1980s and 1990s, first by minority Republicans in the early 1990s and then by the minority Democrats after the 1994 elections. In the period between 2007 and 2014, when the Republicans were back in the minority, obstructionism redoubled.

It was inevitable that partisan polarization and Senate minority obstruc-

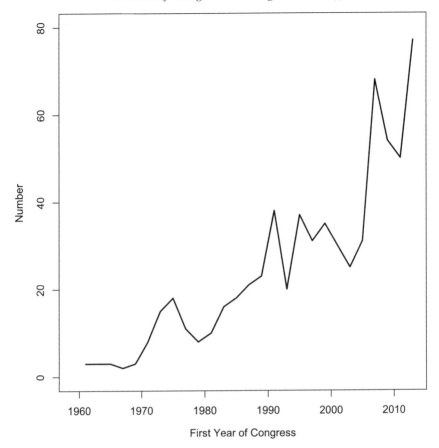

Fig. 2.3. Number of cloture petitions filed on bills, 1961–2014. (Compiled by the authors from the official Senate website [http://www.senate.gov/pagelayout/reference/cloture_motions/clotureCounts.htm].)

tionism would influence how majority leaders and bill managers pursue resolving differences between House and Senate versions of legislation. Until 2013, the Senate had to adopt three motions to get to conference: a motion that the Senate insist on its amendments to a House bill (or disagree to the House amendments to a Senate bill), a motion to request a conference with the House, and a motion to authorize the presiding officer to appoint conferees. In most cases, these motions were wrapped into one unanimous consent request. If a senator objected to such a request, she or he could force a cloture vote on each of the three motions. If cloture was invoked, senators could force the full post-cloture debate on each motion and compel their colleagues to endure a lengthy delay in sending a bill to conference. As discussed in more detail below, filibuster reforms in 2013 streamlined the process of going to conference by combining the three conference motions.

Once a conference report is ready for debate in the Senate, it too can be filibustered. Bills that have made it to and through conference generally would be expected to attract enough support for cloture, but there have been many occasions when a filibuster of a conference report has proven to be a problem for the majority. Still, a conference offers a distinct benefit for a majority leader or bill manager since conference reports cannot be amended. This can be important to resolving differences with the House and paving the way for Senate approval of the conference report. It also allows bill managers to accept a variety of provisions during initial Senate floor consideration of a bill and later strip them from the bill in conference without concern that the conference report will face amendments to restore them (Van Houweling 2006).

Because filibusters of conference motions and conference reports were not a problem until the 1990s, going to conference was the preferred option for majority leaders and bill managers for complex, controversial bills. The first cloture petition filed on a conference report occurred in 1970, but over the next two decades only seven bills were associated with cloture petitions on their conference reports. In 1991–1992 (102nd Congress), the Democratic majority leader filed cloture petitions on seven conference reports to expedite business when confronted with Republican delaying tactics. All of these cloture efforts succeeded or proved unnecessary and were withdrawn, but in 1994, for the first time, cloture failed on a campaign finance reform bill when minority Republicans filibustered the conference report. The Republicans made the majority party's incompetence in running Congress a major theme in their campaign and backed it up by pointing to the dearth of legislation passed. Republicans, of course, won House and Senate majorities in the 1994 elections.

The lessons of 1994 registered with senators. Minority senators could tie the Senate in procedural knots and blame the majority. Overall, the toll from minority obstruction of conference motions and conference reports during the 1990s was at least a half dozen bills blocked and killed (Rybicki 2003; Sinclair 2012a).

Despite the intensifying partisan conflict over conferences, Senate conference delegations, usually composed of most members of the committees originating legislation, continued to involve minority party members in meaningful ways. That changed after the turn of the new century. After Republicans regained a slim Senate majority in the 2002 elections, they excluded Democrats from meaningful participation on several conferences, which Democrats claimed motivated them to become more obstructionist on conference motions and reports. This came to a head in late 2003, when Democrats blocked motions to go to conference on prominent bills to protest their treatment in previous conferences. Minority Leader Tom Daschle (D-SD) announced that "we're going to insist that we be full partners or we're not going to have a conference at all" (Allen and Cochran 2003, 2761).

Later in that Congress, Democrats, who accused the Republicans of continued mistreatment, refused to cooperate with conference proceedings. In one instance, they refused to help form a quorum for the conference to meet. In another, they refused consent to have conferees appointed to a conference. In both cases, prior to sending the bills to conference, Democrats insisted on a bipartisan agreement among senators that certain provisions in the Senate versions would not be modified in conference without their participation. In the first case, Majority Whip Mitch McConnell (R-KY), declared: "What [the Democrats] are doing is saying that 41 of us will deny you the ability to go to conference unless we get to write the final bill. . . . It is simply unacceptable and will not be allowed" (Preston 2004). Daschle's response to all of this was the observation that "realistically, the most important thing we can get done next year is elect a Democratic majority in November" (Cochran 2004, 12).

In this context, the formal use of a conference committee became less important. Party interests, more than committee jurisdiction or the interests of individual legislators to be involved, became the dominant concern. The *New York Times* chief congressional correspondent observed, in a piece subtitled "Process Undone by Partisanship":

> The congressional conference committee, vaguely familiar to generations of Americans from their battered civics texts, is in danger of losing its prominent role in how a bill becomes law.
>
> Once the penultimate stage in the life of any bill as a forum for House and Senate members to work out their differences, the conference committee has fallen on hard times, shoved aside in the last five years by partisanship and legislative expediency. As a result, there is often no public scrutiny of the last-minute compromises that produce a law.
>
> The preferred alternative revolves around informal meetings mainly among senior Democratic lawmakers, who gather to cut a final deal and then bat the finished product back and forth between

the House and Senate until it is approved. It is a makeshift process that has come to be known as ping-ponging. (Hulse 2007, 1)

As an alternative to using a conference committee, majority party leaders could instead

- choose to work out House-Senate differences before acting on the legislation so that a fresh bill could be adopted without post-passage actions required;
- have one house adopt compromise language as an amendment to the other house's bill and return it to the first house for final approval; or
- incorporate the provisions of the negotiated bill into another bill that is in conference (an airdrop, in congressional jargon).

These alternatives were used with increasing frequency in the first decade of the new century (Allison 2004; Beth et al. 2009; Sinclair 2012a).

Majority Leader Bill Frist (R-TN), who took over for Lott in 2003, pursued non-conference strategies frequently. Predictably, Democrats complained about being excluded from the process and, whenever the few conferences were appointed, having no meaningful role. After gaining a majority in the House and Senate in the 2006 elections, Democrats made some efforts to correct the situation. Harry Reid wrote the new Republican leader, Mitch McConnell, that he intended to convene "real" conference committees with minority participation (Kady 2006).[3] The Democratic leader's commitment to reinvigorating the conference process proved shallow (Hulse 2007). Of course, this is not something a Senate leader can really promise because intercameral processes have to be arranged with House leadership. Reid, like Frist, found that efficiency and working around the minority served the interests of his party (Wolfensberger 2008).

Frist and Reid went a step farther than merely avoiding conference. When the majority leader fills the amendment tree in conjunction with invoking cloture on a House amendment to a Senate bill or amendment, she or he eliminates the opportunity for the opposition to offer amendments and delay a vote on the House amendment. Thus, in combination with cloture, a majority leader's decision to exchange amendments between the houses and fill the amendment tree can streamline the process of resolving House-Senate differences, and minimizes the opportunities for votes on unfriendly or politically sensitive amendments.

If the majority leader can acquire 60 votes for cloture at each stage, these tactics tighten a majority leader's grip on floor action. The leader can fill the amendment tree before and after cloture and then get an up-or-down vote on her or his version of the bill without votes on amendments. The leader can then invoke cloture on a conference report (or on a House amendment), followed by filling the amendment tree, to acquire an up-or-down vote on a House-Senate compromise she or he favors. Effectively, this process makes House amendments non-amendable, like conference reports, which encourages the use of an exchange of amendments and avoids the creation of a conference committee.[4]

Frist appears to have been the first majority leader to fill the tree on a House amendment, doing so twice (Beth et al. 2009). Reid did so more frequently—at least eight times in his first three years as majority leader. The net result: less minority participation, less transparent deliberations, and fewer conference committees.

Perhaps the best known instance of avoiding conference to circumvent a filibuster occurred during the passage of the Affordable Care Act ("Obamacare") discussed at the outset of this chapter. In short, with the death of Senator Ted Kennedy (D-MA), and his subsequent replacement with a Republican, the Senate Democratic majority found themselves short of the 60 votes needed to overcome a filibuster of a conference report or House amendment to the Senate version. Informal negotiations between House and Senate majority party Democrats resolved differences between the chambers' bills, and the resulting legislation was treated as a new reconciliation bill. The reconciliation bill was subject to a debate limit, as provided in the Budget Act, and so was not filibustered in the Senate. The House adopted the Senate bill and the reconciliation bill modified that law. Obamacare, as a result, was two bills, not one, and each bill was formally adopted without a conference or amendments between the houses.

Frustration with minority obstruction on motions to go to conference led the Senate to adopt a new rule in 2013. The rule combined the three motions to go to conference with the House (to disagree or insist, to request a conference, and to authorize the appointment of conferees) into one motion. Debate on a cloture motion related to such a conference motion is limited to two hours and, if the cloture motion is adopted, no further debate on the conference motion is allowed. The rule does not appear to have discouraged threats to block action on conference reports.

The 2010s

While the House and Senate followed different paths, by the time the Republicans had assumed majorities in both chambers following the 2014 elections, the parties had taken over post-passage action from committees

on most major legislation. Avoiding filibusters became difficult, and usually impossible, in the Senate due to the intensity of the partisan competition and polarization, so avoiding conference became a central feature of
majority party strategies. Committee leaders remain involved in most steps
of the process, but their involvement often is highly constrained by the
expectations of their parties and leaders. Indeed, party conflict has made
Senate action very difficult and interchamber negotiations stressful and
delicate. Likewise, partisan tensions in the House led rank-and-file members to delegate increasing authority over post-passage decision making
to party leaders. Fewer bills are passed and party-based negotiations often
yield legislation that circumvents the traditional conference process.

These patterns, repeated in each of the last half dozen Congresses, have
changed expectations. The assumption made by most legislators going into
each recent Congress is that battle lines will be drawn by the parties, the
minority will do whatever it can to obstruct the majority, and the majority
will exclude the minority from important deliberations. This situation sets
majority party goals for legislative productivity very low, particularly in the
Senate. When party control of the House, Senate, and president is divided,
stalemate is expected on many issues. Behavior adjusts accordingly—few
serious proposals are made, judgments about what is feasible move from
committee rooms to leadership offices, and attention drifts to winning seats
in the next election. When the House and Senate manage to act on legislation, usually some must-pass bills, they do so under severe time constraints
and with sensitive party interests at stake. Party interests overwhelm the
interests of committees and legislators who favor the traditional ways of
resolving House-Senate differences.

More Evidence

We have described two waves of change in post-passage politics. The first
wave was marked by the reforms to the House committee system in the
1970s as well as the introduction of multi-committee bills. This wave altered
post-passage practices for about 20 years. It represented a new but temporary
equilibrium in balancing the interests of committees, the majority party, and
individual legislators. The second wave was a by-product of intensifying partisanship and the emergence of a more party-oriented and less committee-
oriented legislative process in the 1990s. Its effects are still being felt today.
In this section, we examine the historical patterns in the use of post-passage
methods to more clearly see the consequences of these changes.

The Move to Larger, Structured Conferences

The changes in committee politics and the budget process that were produced by Democratic majorities in the 1970s set the stage for fewer but larger, more complex conferences committees in the years that followed. Committee and party leaders were confronted with new challenges in naming and structuring conference delegations, and several innovations followed. The typical structure for a conference delegation that includes limited-purpose conferees is to match limited-purpose conferees to the titles or sections that fall under the jurisdiction of different standing committees. If there is a lead committee, as there is in the case of a reconciliation bill, general-purpose conferees usually are drawn from that committee.

We label conference delegations with at least one limited-purpose conferee as "complex," and label as "simple" the traditional conference delegation comprised exclusively of general-purpose conferees. Figure 2.4 reports the frequency of simple and complex conference delegations in the House and Senate for the period since the mid-1960s. Complex conferences were used with considerable frequency for the first time in the 95th House (1977–1978), the first Congress of Tip O'Neill's speakership. Speaker O'Neill used multiple referrals more frequently and was more responsive than his predecessor to demands for expanding conference delegations (Smith 1989).

Three patterns visible in figure 2.4 deserve attention. First, in both houses the sharp decline in the number of conferences that took place in the early 1980s was at the expense of simple conference delegations. A reasonable (and correct) hypothesis is that complex conferences, and more generally multiply referred bills, substituted for many of the bills that otherwise would have been subject to simple conferences. This is not the whole story, particularly for the Senate, but fewer and larger measures being resolved in complex conferences is a significant part of it.

However, with the declining number of conferences, it is important to note that the frequencies of simple and complex delegations were not merely the inverse of one another. The correlation between simple and complex conferences from the 95th (1977–1978) to 103rd (1993–1994) Congresses is negative (-0.28 for the House and -0.22 for the Senate), and so there is some evidence that complex conferences came at the expense of simple conferences. But the relationship is far from one of perfect replacement, in which simple conferences merely became complex ones. The pattern of larger and fewer bills appears to have also played a central role in limiting the number of simple delegations. Since the Republi-

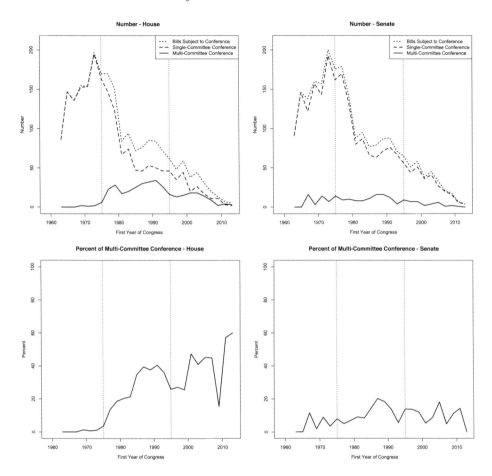

Fig. 2.4. Number and percentage of simple and complex conferences, 1963–2014. (Compiled by the authors from *Calendars of the United States House of Representatives and History of Legislation, Final Edition*, 88th Congress–113th Congress.)

cans gained majority party status in both houses in the 1994 elections, the overall number of conferences of both types fell and the correlation between the number of conferences of the two types actually switched to being positive for the few remaining conferences (0.73 for the House and 0.87 for the Senate).

Second, since the mid-1970s, the House has used complex delegations more than the Senate. By the end of 1980s, over one-third of House conference delegations had a complex structure. In the Congresses of the twenty-first century, the percentage of House conferences that were complex exceeded 40 in all but one Congress. In fact, complex conferences accounted for over half of all conferences in the 112th (four of seven) and 113th (three of five) Congresses (2011–2012, 2013–2014, respectively). In contrast, the Senate has used complex conferences infrequently, even when membership for a conference delegation is drawn from multiple committees.

Third, complex conferences varied in size but they were quite big for the period in which there existed a negative relationship between the frequencies of complex and simple conferences (95th–103rd Congress). In general, general-purpose conferees may or may not constitute a majority of the total number of conferees assigned to a part of the bill. But, in some instances, the number of separate voting groups, or subconferences, that comprise a single conference committee can be substantial, as can be the number of limited-purpose conferees assigned to a particular subconference.

The Omnibus Budget Reconciliation Act of 1981 demonstrates how complicated conference committees became. Given the expansiveness of the bill, the House and Senate both appointed a large number of limited-purpose conferees. In the end, the House appointed a total of 186 conferees and the Senate appointed 70, 43 percent and 70 percent of the entire membership of their respective bodies. Moreover, this conference committee consisted of 37 House subconferences (10 general-purpose conferees from the Budget Committee and 36 limited-purpose subconferences), and 16 Senate subconferences (7 general-purpose conferees from the Budget Committee and 15 limited-purpose subconferences).

Table 2.1 lists the largest conference committees during the period of analysis. Specifically, the list contains all conferences that had at least 20 subconferences or 100 conferees in the House, and it lists the conferences in (decreasing) order of their number of subconferences. All the bills with the largest conferences are from the 1977–94 period, when Democrats were in the House majority and were quite inclusive in appointing a conference on multi-committee bills. Just over a third of the bills on the list are budget reconciliation bills and another third are defense authorization bills. Chapter 4 provides a more detailed story on these important bills.

The Decline of Conferences

The move to fewer but larger bills since the 1970s was given additional impetus in the last two decades by partisan stalemate and the need to pass

TABLE 2.1. The largest complex conference committees

Congress	Bill	Bill Title	House		Senate	
			#Subconferences	#Conferees	#Subconferences	#Conferees
100	HR3	Omnibus Trade and Competitiveness Act of 1987	81	155	11	44
101	S2830	Food, Agriculture, Conservation, and Trade Act of 1990	58	116	1	7
103	HR2264	Omnibus Budget Reconciliation Act of 1993	46	165	13	51
97	HR3982	Omnibus Budget Reconciliation Act of 1981	37	186	16	70
99	HR3128	Omnibus Budget Reconciliation Act of 1985	29	177	18	61
101	HR3299	Omnibus Budget Reconciliation Act of 1989	28	169	11	57
101	HR5835	Omnibus Budget Reconciliation Act of 1990	28	67	12	52
100	HR3545	Omnibus Budget Reconciliation Act of 1987	27	140	13	59
102	HR776	Energy Policy Act of 1992	27	102	8	32
103	HR2401	National Defense Authorization Act for Fiscal Year 1994	26	111	1	20
102	HR5006	National Defense Authorization Act for Fiscal Year 1993	26	141	1	21
99	HR5300	Omnibus Budget Reconciliation Act of 1986	24	108	15	53
104	HR1530	National Defense Authorization Act for Fiscal Year 1996	23	83	1	21
99	HR2100	Food Security Act of 1985	22	53	1	9
102	HR11	Revenue Act of 1992	22	73	2	16

TABLE 2.1.—*Continued*

Congress	Bill	Bill Title	House		Senate	
			#Subconferences	#Conferees	#Subconferences	#Conferees
104	HR3230	National Defense Authorization Act for Fiscal Year 1997	20	75	1	21
106	HR4205	National Defense Authorization Act for Fiscal Year 2001	20	75	1	19
101	HR4739	National Defense Authorization Act for Fiscal Year 1991	19	134	1	20
101	S1630	Clean Air Act Amendments of 1990	19	130	2	9
101	HR2461	National Defense Authorization Act for Fiscal Years 1990 and 1991	18	101	1	17

Note: This list includes all the bills that have more than 20 subconferences or 100 conferees assigned by the House.

Source: Compiled by the authors from *Calendars of the United States House of Representatives and History of Legislation, Final Edition*, 88th Congress–113th Congress.

omnibus bills to overcome gridlock. Naturally, this pattern reduced the number of bills that would normally be resolved in conference. However, the partisan divide that created the need for omnibus legislating also made passing measures by regular order more difficult, particularly in the Senate. This further reduced the number of bills going to conference, and led majority party leaders to find non-conference methods to pass legislation.

These developments are visible in figure 2.5, which documents the number of enacted laws that went through conference, were adopted through an exchange of amendments between the houses, or had been subject to both a conference report and an exchange of amendments. Consistent with our observations at the beginning of this chapter, the *number* of bills subject to one or both of these post-passage methods declined since the 1970s as bill size increased but passage declined. As a percentage of all enacted bills, however, the conferencing method remained at 50 percent or more until the most recent Congresses. In recent years, as the 2009 Affordable Care Act case demonstrates, majority party leaders have avoided conferences as much as possible. To some extent, the exchange of amendments between the houses has served as a substitute for conference. However, avoiding debatable and amendable vehicles became the preferred route of majority

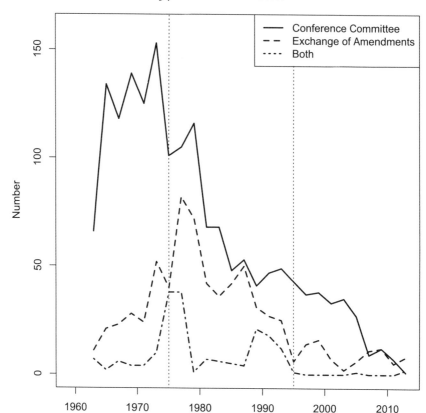

Fig. 2.5. Number of public laws, by House-Senate reconciliation method, 1963–2014. (Compiled by the authors from *CQ Almanac*.)

leaders in some cases, which reduced the use of both formal post-passage methods. During recent Congresses, in which partisan competition is at historically high levels, party leaders are simply less inclined to leave the details of post-passage bargaining to chance.

Major and Partisan Measures

To take another slice at the record, we consider whether the traditional view of conferences—that they were required for large, complex bills—still fits current practice. In this traditional view of congressional decision making, major bills tend to generate partisan divisions and the complexities can be successfully negotiated only through lengthy conference negotiations.

Much of what we have reported challenges that view. Figure 2.6 shows the trends in the use of post-passage methods in two ways, by the importance of the legislation in the top panel and by the presence or absence of a party vote in the bottom panel.

For the top panel, we place legislation that became law in three categories based on the space in *CQ Almanac* that is devoted to the bill.[5] It is considered to be "highly important" if the length in column lines in *CQ Almanac* is greater than its median value (125 lines), "somewhat important" if the bill is discussed in *CQ Almanac* but under the median for length of coverage, and "least important" if the bill is not covered in *CQ Almanac*. There is little trend and a low frequency of conferencing for bills in the somewhat and least important categories. The trend for important bills follows the pattern we have shown in the aggregate—a fairly steady decline in the use of conferences for important bills since the 1970s.

For the bottom panel, we identify bills that were subject to a "party vote" on final passage in the House.[6] A party vote is a vote on which a majority of Democrats oppose a majority of Republicans. Bills subject to partisan divisions go to conference more frequently than other bills, but the difference is not large. It is important to see that, even as party voting has become more common and the number of bills enacted has reached historic lows, the percentage of bills subject to a partisan divide that have gone to conference fell to very low levels in recent Congresses.

Multivariate Estimates

To determine whether committee of origin, partisan context, and the importance of the legislation have independent effects on post-passage processes, we report estimates of multivariate models. We introduce two models to explore the factors that influence (1) the decision whether or not to use conference, and (2) the structure of conference when conferences are used. The dependent variable for the first model is a dichotomous measure that is coded 1 for bills that went to conference and 0 for bills that were resolved by another method, using all bills that became public law between 1963 and 2010. The second model then examines the subset of bills that went to conference and became public law during this period. The dependent variable for this model is a dichotomous measure that is coded 1 for complex conferences—those conferences with at least one limited-purpose conferee—and is coded 0 for simple conferences—those conferences having exclusively general-purpose conferees.

We include an identical set of independent variables in both models to

Importance of Legislation

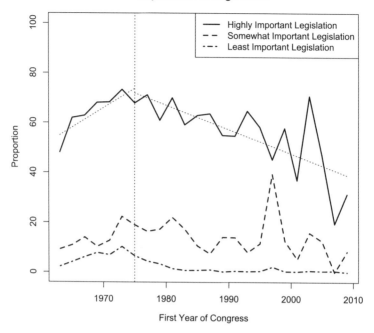

Types of Roll Call Voting

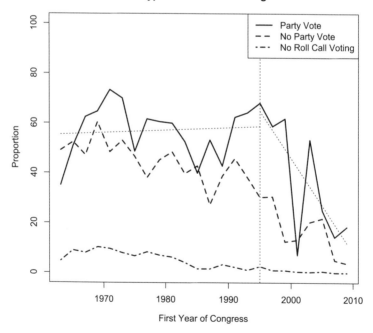

Fig. 2.6. Percent of public laws going to conference, by importance and party vote, 1963–2010. (Compiled by the authors from Policy Agendas Project [for importance of legislation] and Political Institutions and Public Choice Roll-Call Database [for party vote].)

capture theoretically important aspects of the parent standing committees, the legislation under consideration, and the partisan environment within which the post-passage decision is being made. With respect to standing committee characteristics, we include three indicator variables to account for whether the House standing committee of origin was a prestige committee, a policy committee, or a constituency committee, using Deering and Smith's (1997) standing committee typology.[7] We also account for the bias present in the standing committee of origin by measuring the difference in common-space DW-NOMINATE scores between the standing committee and chamber medians, such that positive values indicate pro-majority-party bias (i.e., the standing committee median is located on the majority party side of the chamber median) and negative values indicate minority party bias.

In addition, we include several variables that account for variation in the importance and policy content of the given legislation. We, again, use the measure of importance, introduced above, that draws upon the amount of space devoted to the bill in the *CQ Almanac*. Therefore, we include three indicator variables measuring whether the bill was least, somewhat, or highly important. Similarly, we can infer something about the salience and content of the given bill from the resulting vote that occurred on final passage. In particular, bills that are dispensed with by voice vote tend to be either non-controversial or of minimal visibility, or (likely) both. More divisive and important legislation tends to receive a recorded vote (Lynch and Madonna 2013). Yet, bills that generate party votes, in which a majority of one party votes in opposition to a majority of the other, are often viewed as being most central to the parties, since they signal core differences between the parties (Poole and Rosenthal 2007). To account for these various scenarios, we include three indicator variables for bills decided by voice vote, recorded non-party votes, and party votes. We also account for the policy content of bills by including indicator variables for three policy areas that are theoretically important to post-passage decision making—appropriations, budget, and taxes. Budget and tax policies are coded using the Policy Agendas Project's subtopic code to identify measures relating to the "National Budget" and "Tax Code," respectively. Appropriations policy is coded on the basis of the standing committee of origin using the same Policy Agendas Project's database, where we require the bill to originate in the Appropriations Committee of at least one of the chambers.

Finally, we include two variables to account for the partisan environment within which the bill is being considered. The first such variable measures polarization using the method introduced in chapter 1 and used by Vander Wielen and Smith (2011). This measure incorporates interparty hetero- geneity and intraparty homogeneity in a single measure, with increasing values representing growing polarization. We also include a variable that measures the majority party's seat advantage, measured as the proportion of the seats held by the majority party. During the period of analysis, this variable ranges in values from 0.51 in the 107th Congress (2001–2002) to 0.68 in the 89th Congress (1965–1966).

Given that the bills included in both models are nested within Con- gresses, we estimate multilevel logistic regression models with random intercepts to permit the membership to have different baseline propensi- ties to use conferences (in model 1) and use complex conference struc- tures (in model 2) across Congresses. The resulting standard deviation of the random intercepts indicates the amount of variation in this propen- sity across Congresses, with larger values indicating greater variation. The results of this analysis are presented in table 2.2.

The results reported in the first column of table 2.2 demonstrate the pattern of conference use. In terms of standing-committee-specific factors, we find some evidence that conferences have historically been more widely used to resolve differences on legislation originating in prestige commit- tees. This is likely the result of prestige committees having jurisdictional authority over comparatively complex and important legislation, in con- junction with having a membership that is typically more representative of chamber preferences than other types of committees (Vander Wielen and Smith 2011), making conference an efficient and palatable means of resolving intercameral differences. However, we find no evidence that pol- icy committees or committee bias have a statistically discernible effect on the use of conference.

We find considerably more evidence that bill attributes play a central role in the post-passage decision making: important and partisan measures are statistically more likely to go to conference than other legislation, all else equal. Figure 2.7 shows the predicted probabilities of conference use along with their corresponding confidence intervals for bills of varying importance and vote types.[8] We find that highly important legislation, using our measure, is approximately 11 times more likely to go to confer- ence compared to the least important legislation (predicted probabilities of 0.35 and 0.03, respectively). Moreover, highly important bills have a statis- tically higher likelihood of going to conference than somewhat important bills. Bills that receive party votes are roughly 5 times more likely to go to conference than those considered by voice vote (predicted probabilities of 0.18 and 0.04, respectively), although we do not find evidence of a statistical difference in the likelihood of conference across the types of recorded votes (i.e., party and non-party votes). Beyond bill importance and partisanship, we find evidence that enacted appropriations bills have, on average, had a higher likelihood of going to conference, while budget bills have been less likely to go to conference. We give special attention to these categories of bills in chapter 4.

The evidence is compelling that polarization has led to a marked decline in the use of conference. Figure 2.8 (upper panel) shows the predicted probability of using conference across the range of our polarization measure, holding all other variables at their means. The predicted

TABLE 2.2. Multivariate multilevel logit models for use and structure of conference committees

	Going to Conference	Simple vs. Complex Conference
Standing committee type		
- Constituency committee *(omitted)*		
- Policy committee	−0.0881 (−0.81)	−0.5138 (−1.60)
- Prestige committee	0.3719* (2.10)	−0.8246 (−1.75)
Standing committee bias	0.7794 (1.38)	−0.2315 (−0.14)
Important bill		
- Least important *(omitted)*		
- Somewhat important	0.9980* (8.76)	0.4968 (1.04)
- Highly important	2.7786* (25.52)	1.0233* (2.38)
Vote type		
- No roll call vote *(omitted)*		
- Roll call but no party vote	1.5135* (15.39)	1.1955* (3.29)
- Party vote	1.7424* (12.24)	1.5798* (3.88)
Policy domain		
- Appropriations	1.4816* (8.06)	−3.4966* (−7.04)
- Budget	−0.6870* (-2.07)	1.0659 (1.43)
- Tax	−0.0735 (-0.23)	−1.0258 (−1.11)
- Others *(omitted)*		
Congress-level partisan environment		
- Polarization	−0.6096* (−6.21)	1.9354* (4.48)
- Majority party size	−2.6171 (−1.49)	4.3212 (0.52)
Constant	−0.0527 (−0.04)	−13.1542* (−2.12)
SD Constant	0.2521	1.3019
N	9,380	1,426
Log Likelihood	−2125.6	−318.0
Bayesian Information Criterion	4,379.2	737.6
Groups	24	24

Note: Unit of analysis is a public law; dependent variable for the first column is 1 if conference is used and 0 otherwise; dependent variable for the second column is 1 if complex conference is used and 0 if simple conference is used (public laws enacted without conference are excluded from the latter model). Coefficients are shown with *z*-values in parenthesis; *p < 0.05

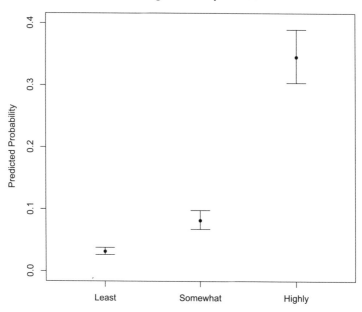

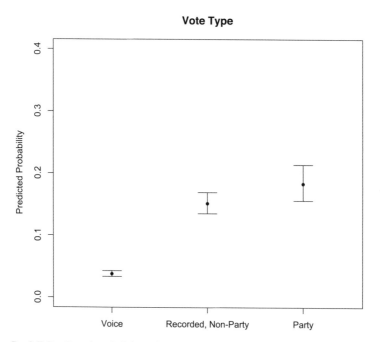

Fig. 2.7. Predicted probability of going to conference, by importance and party vote. (Note: Predicted probabilities are calculated for three different types, holding other independent variables at their mean values.)

probability of an average bill being resolved in conference drops from approximately 0.09 at the minimum of polarization during the period of analysis (in the 90th Congress) to roughly 0.02 at the maximum (in the 109th Congress). This is all the more impressive when considering that general time trends are accounted for via the multilevel structure of the model, in which we find consistently smaller/negative intercepts in recent Congresses. And when looking at the effects of polarization across varying levels of bill importance, the results are even more striking (shown in the bottom panel of figure 2.8). Since the predicted probabilities are generated by a non-linear (logit) model, variation in the level of bill importance has implications for the rate of change in the probability of conference across the polarization interval. In particular, we find a dramatic difference in the rate of decline across the various levels of bill importance, with highly important bills experiencing the largest marginal decline and the least important bills the smallest. Specifically, the predicted probability of going to conference for highly important bills falls by 0.34 from the lowest to highest levels of polarization, whereas the analogous decline in predicted probability is merely 0.04 for the least important bills. This finding is consistent with the notion that party polarization is at the center of the demise of conference committees, since we would expect the effects of polarization to be most pronounced on the legislation that is most central to the parties' legislative records. Varying the vote types tells a similar story with respect to polarization.

The second column of table 2.2 shows the estimates for the model examining the use of simple versus complex conferences. On average, important and partisan legislation is more likely to go to a complex conference. This offers some confirmation that complex conferences were an innovation that served partisan motivations. We also find that appropriations bills, most of which are produced by one appropriations committee in each house, are consistently more likely to go to simple conference.

Finally, the results suggest that partisan polarization played an important role in the determination of conference structure across time: there is a positive, and statistically meaningful, relationship between polarization and the use of complex conferences. With the rising levels of internal cohesiveness and interparty differences that characterized the 1970s, the House Democratic majority pushed for wider participation in conferences, prompting larger conferences with more creative jurisdictional arrangements. Figure 2.9 shows the predicted probability of using a complex conference across the range of polarization during the period of analysis. For an average bill, the predicted probability of using a complex conference

Polarization

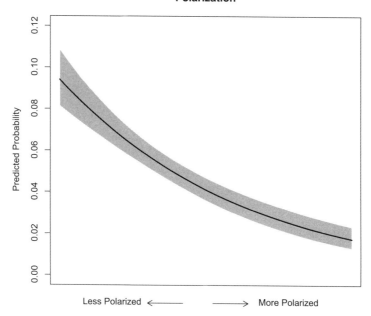

Polarization and Importance

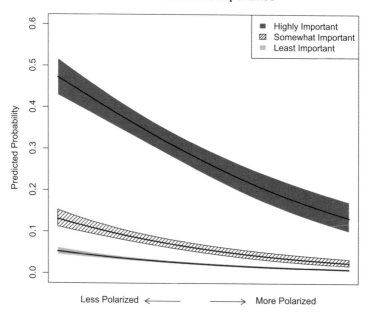

Fig. 2.8. Predicted probability of going to conference, by polarization. (Note: Predicted probabilities are calculated for different levels of polarization, holding other independent variables at their mean values.)

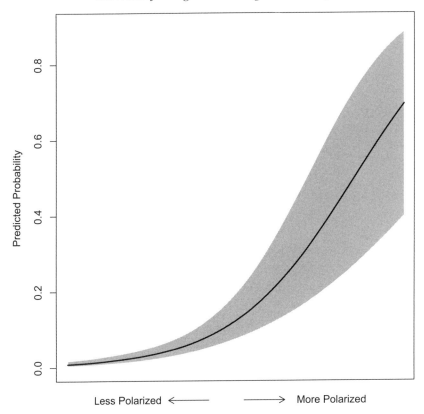

Fig. 2.9. Predicted probability of going to complex conference, by polarization. (Note: Predicted probabilities are calculated for different levels of polarization, holding other independent variables at their mean values.)

increases by approximately 0.69 when increasing polarization from its minimum to maximum values. The size of the confidence interval increases considerably for extremely high values of polarization due to the dearth of conferences in the recent period of intense polarization.

Conclusion

Dramatic changes have occurred in post-passage politics in Congress. The first wave of change was a response to both factionalism within the House majority party and partisan conflict. It involved expanding the range of House committees and members involved in conferences. This wave was propelled by liberal Democrats in the House who wanted to place policy outcomes more in line with the views of most Democrats. Simultaneously, the invention of multi-committee measures, both in and out of the budget domain, allowed wider participation in deliberations over major bills. The second wave was a by-product of partisan warfare and led to a radical reduction in the use of conferences to resolve House-Senate differences.

These developments in post-passage politics conform to larger patterns in congressional policy making. Partisan competition for control of the House and Senate and the polarization of the parties shape the political environment of congressional policy making in basic ways. When one party is in no short-term danger of losing majority control and when the parties' policy differences are modest, the policy-making processes tends to be centered in committees. Party leaders serve to facilitate the passage of committee-written legislation, and a conference-based, committee-oriented process characterizes efforts to reconcile House-Senate differences on major legislation. When partisanship is intense because of keen electoral competition between the parties or sharply polarized policy views, committees take a back seat to parties and their leaders, and methods to reconcile House-Senate differences are chosen based on the needs of majority parties.

Moreover, the rules of the legislative process condition the effects of partisan conflict on legislating. Intense partisanship has the most conspicuous effect in the Senate, where the minority is then motivated to obstruct majority action and the majority responds by looking to limit the opportunity for filibusters. Changes in the rules, such as the creation of the budget process rules in 1974, can eventually alter strategies and facilitate outcomes that otherwise would not favor the majority so strongly.

THREE

The Bias from Post-Passage Politics

With the sweeping changes in congressional policy making that have accompanied the rise of strong partisanship, it is natural to wonder whether partisan biases in post-passage processes have deepened, too. We have given the most important answer by observing how a process that was once dominated by committee leaders and conference committees is now dominated by party leaders and non-conference methods for resolving House-Senate differences. In recent Congresses, the minority party has little role in post-passage deliberations in either house. The process could hardly be more biased in favor of the interests of the majority party.

It is important to understand the context of these recent developments. The nearly complete disappearance of conference committees is a very recent phenomenon, one that is regretted by many legislators and may be short-lived. A key component of that context is the nature of partisan bias generated by conference committees, which is the subject of this chapter. An explicit purpose of House reforms of the 1970s was to make majority party conferees more representative of the party, but this effect has not been fully evaluated in previous studies.

While exploring the advantage the majority party acquires in the conference process, we give special attention to complex conferences with both general- and limited-purpose conferees. As we have seen, the emergence of multi-committee bills in the 1970s yielded more conference delegations with specialized conferees, but the effect of this development on the bias of conferees has not been studied. We consider the differences between the two types of conferees and the bias of subconferences composed of both types to evaluate the effect of complex conferences on majority party bias.

We find a long-standing pattern of a pro-majority-party bias in the ideological composition of conference committees. Since the mid-1970s, conferees, on balance, have exhibited ideological leanings that favored the majority party, even beyond the bias of their parent committees. This was true under both Democratic and Republican majorities. The bias is visible in the Senate, too, but it is not quite a strong or consistent as in the House.

Critically, the pro-majority bias does *not* bring conference delegation medians all the way to the majority party median, at least on average. In fact, in every Congress since the mid-1970s, House and Senate conference delegations exhibit an average median liberal-conservative score that is more moderate than the median of the majority party. The difference is small, but it suggests that, in recent decades, a party-oriented process is likely to yield more extreme outcomes than the more traditional committee-oriented, conference-based process that has evaporated.

Understanding Conference Delegation Bias

The study of bias in the committee system has a long pedigree in political science. Political scientists observed years ago that standing committees are created by their parent chambers and must have their legislative recommendations approved by the parent bodies, but they have emphasized that committee members may be attuned to narrower interests. Committee members and leaders are effectively appointed by their parties so committee members have at least some incentive to meet their party colleagues' expectations. Moreover, legislators have good political reasons to give attention to the concerns of their constituents, and particularly the organized interests, in their home states and districts. The political science of congressional politics yielded a variety of insights about the conditions under which the parent chamber, parties, and external constituencies took an interest in, and influenced, committee policy making (see, e.g., Fenno 1973; Krehbiel 1991; Maltzman 1997; Shepsle and Weingast 1987; Deering and Smith 1997).

During the middle decades of the twentieth century, committees were viewed as part of a pluralistic, decentralized policy-making process in the federal government. Legislators represent widely different constituencies, but in many states and districts there are particularly important interests—agriculture, manufacturing, unions, education, military bases, tourism, and so on. In the pluralistic politics of the mid-twentieth century, legislators were attracted to committees that had jurisdiction over one or more of their constituencies' primary interests and the associated executive departments and agencies. Policy, which originates in legislation and agency rules, usually was heavily influenced by the policy views of committee members and the organized private interests that lobbied them and supported their reelection campaigns. Party leaders did not play a significant role on most issues, and presidents focused only on a handful of the most important issues.

As we outlined in previous chapters, the 1970s brought the assertion of greater majority party control over the affairs of House standing committees, which has intensified in the years since then. At first, this meant expanding the size of conference delegations so that Democrats could enjoy conference delegations that were more representative of the party (that is, more liberal) than was often the case in preceding decades. As figure 3.1 shows, the mean number of House conferees moved up from 5.86 in the mid-1960s to 11.49 in the late 1970s. Senate practice did not change much at the same time, although a more modest expansion of conference delegations occurred there, too.

An open question is how much partisan bias was introduced when House Democratic liberals pushed for better representation on conference delegations (Lazarus and Monroe 2007; Vander Wielen and Smith 2011). The bias may be generated in several ways, only some of which involve active intervention by party leaders. Most obvious, the majority party has a built-in advantage by virtue of the long-standing practice of giving each party seats on committees and conference delegations roughly in proportion to its relative size in the chamber as a whole. Even if committee members are a random sample of each party and conferees are a random sample of each party's committee contingent, it is likely that the balance of views on a conference delegation will favor the majority party's views over those of the minority party.

In practice, strict proportionality is difficult to achieve. The precise proportions for the two parties in the parent chambers cannot be replicated in the smaller units. This has given the majority party an opportunity to acquire fractional advantages on most committees and conference delegations, an opportunity that it exploits most of the time. Over recent decades, the majority party has been given a fractional advantage on nearly all committees. In fact, the majority party advantage in the total number of committee seats, compared with the House chamber, averaged 2.1 percent during the 1973–2015 period and stretched to over 3.5 percent under Republican majorities in two Congresses in the 1990s (Glassman and Eckman 2015).

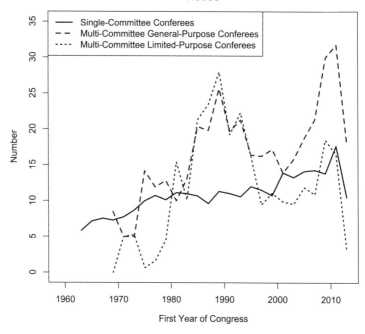

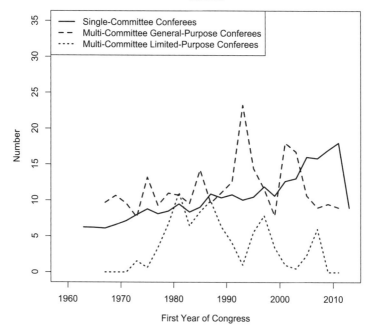

Fig. 3.1. Mean number of conferees, 1963–2014. (Compiled by the authors from *Calendars of the United States House of Representatives and History of Legislation, Final Edition*, 88th Congress–113th Congress.)

For conference delegations, the majority advantage is larger. The majority party's seat share on conferences is reported in table 3.1. During the most recent period reported (104th–113th Congresses, 1995–2013), following the second wave of change, House majorities averaged 52 percent of the chamber seats but held 60 percent of the single-committee conference appointments and well over 60 percent of the general- and limited-purpose conference appointments in complex conferences. The majority party edge was smaller in the Senate.

Beyond this small but systematic advantage for the majority party, additional pro-majority bias can be introduced by the preferences of majority party legislators who are appointed to conferences. If some discretion is exercised by party leaders, and it can be, then we would expect committee leaders, party factions, and individual legislators to appeal to their party leaders to use that discretion in their interest. They do. Just how responsive leaders are to these appeals is difficult to judge, particularly in the aggregate. It is an insiders' game that even the most attentive Capitol Hill journalists seldom write about.

The developments since the 1970s—intensifying interparty competition and deepening party polarization—lead us to expect that leaders have faced stronger demands to make appointments that reflect party interests and to take more initiative to ensure that conference outcomes meet party expectations. And with increasing intraparty cohesion in preferences we would expect party leaders to encounter less effective opposition to the dominant policy interests of the party from fellow partisans. Of course, the majority party, if undivided in its policy preferences, needs to con-

TABLE 3.1. Average majority party seat share on conference committees

		Parent Chamber	Single-Committee Conferences	Multi-Committee Conferences	
				General-Purpose	Limited-Purpose
House	88–93	0.59	0.59		
	94–103	0.61	0.66	0.62	0.63
	104–113	0.52	0.60	0.62	0.66
	All	0.58	0.62	0.62	0.64
Senate	88–93	0.61	0.61		
	94–103	0.57	0.59	0.56	0.57
	104–113	0.54	0.56	0.57	0.69
	All	0.57	0.60	0.57	0.60

Source: Compiled by the authors from *Calendars of the United States House of Representatives and History of Legislation, Final Edition*, 88th Congress–113th Congress.

trol only a majority of its delegation to insist on its position and approve compromises. The majority party in the House or Senate does not require unanimity or even a large majority among the conferees from that chamber; a simple majority will suffice. In a unidimensional policy space, the liberal-conservative world, this means that having the median member of the conference delegation siding with the majority party view is what matters to the party.

The two waves of change in House conference practice that we describe in the previous chapter are visible in figure 3.1. The first wave of change was about bringing House committees and conferences in line with the preferences of most majority party Democrats by expanding conference delegations and moving to more multi-committee bills. In figure 3.1, we see that the number of conferees per delegation doubled between the mid-1960s and late 1970s for single-committee bills, and multi-committee bills were associated with much larger conferences, too.

The second wave, initiated by House Republicans after the 1994 elections, was about partisan efficiency and control. The Republican leadership appointed smaller conference delegations and a somewhat greater fractional advantage for the majority party. Single-committee conferences did not shrink much, if at all, but Republicans appointed much smaller delegations for the more important multi-committee bills than the Democrats had done. That pattern changed after the turn of the century, when Republicans appointed fewer complex conferences and used general-purpose conferees more often, even on multi-committee bills.

The Senate, as figure 3.1 shows, has not followed the same pattern. There is a long-term trend to appointing more conferees to single-committee conferences—the Senate, like the House, became more participatory in formal conference appointments over recent decades. However, there are no partisan differences that parallel those exhibited in the House. For a time, the Republican majority of the early 1980s followed the House in appointing limited-purpose conferees to a few multi-committee bills, but the pattern was inconsistent thereafter. A few outliers of large multi-committee conferences cause temporary spikes in the number of general-purpose conferees, but these are by no means enduring trends.

The developments underlying figure 3.1 suggest that most of the systematic change we can expect in conference delegation bias occurred in the House. Larger conference delegations should have reduced the fractional advantage of the majority parties, but the expanded participation of Democratic liberals in the 1970s and 1980s may have made the Democratic contingents on delegations more representative of the party as a whole. The reduced-size multi-committee delegations and party scrutiny of the appointments under the Republicans may have further pushed delegations in the direction of the majority party. We explore these patterns in this chapter.

Measuring Bias in Conference Delegations

Vander Wielen and Smith (2011) demonstrate that, for single-committee conferences (i.e., conferences with exclusively general-purpose conferees), there is commonly a pro-majority-party bias in the distribution of conferees' revealed policy positions using Common Space scores (Poole 1998). They find evidence that the medians of conference delegations composed of general-purpose conferees are systematically shifted away from the chamber median in the direction of the majority party median. The bias has grown in recent decades, in part due to the rise in partisan polarization, and is more apparent in the House than in the Senate. With delegations split between majority and minority party members, roughly in proportion to party representation in the parent chambers, this bias is attributed both to fractional advantages that the majority party enjoys in the size of the parties' conference delegations and to the strategic considerations made by party and committee leaders in shaping the composition of their party's delegations. Here, we extend that analysis to all conferees, both single- and multi-committee conferees.

A word of caution is required. We consider this analysis exploratory and preliminary. We examine only general liberal-conservative bias in the composition of conference delegations. We do not examine how conference delegations might vary from their parent chambers or parties in other ways. For example, being pro- or anti-subsidies for farmers may not be highly correlated with liberal-conservative differences and yet might be a significant consideration in the appointment of committee and conference members. In fact, there are likely to be many dimensions of conflict in Congress that are relevant to post-passage politics beyond the major liberal-conservative dimension that appears to be relevant to nearly all important legislation in recent decades (Hurwitz, Moiles, and Rohde 2001; Roberts, Smith, and Haptonstahl 2016). We limit ourselves to the main dimension of partisan conflict—the liberal-conservative dimension.

Measuring Policy Locations

We take advantage of Common Space DW-NOMINATE scores.[1] The common space scales place the House and Senate in the same two-dimensional space based on the assumption that legislators who served in both bodies held the same policy positions in both houses and each legislator kept the same location throughout her or his career in Congress. These are strong assumptions, to be sure, but they allow for direct comparisons across Congresses and between the House and Senate. None of our inferences would substantively change if we used standard DW-NOMINATE scores, which impose a linear trend on a legislator's scores over her or his service in one house. We report results using the first-dimension common space scores that vary in value from -1.0 to +1.0, which is commonly interpreted as measuring a legislator's location on a liberal-to-conservative continuum. We will call this the liberal-conservative score.

Our primary measure of policy locations for the two houses, parties, committees, and conference delegations is the common space score on the liberal-conservative dimension associated with the median member of the relevant body. The median is convenient because, in a unidimensional policy space with all legislators seeking to acquire an outcome as close to their ideal policy outcome as possible, the median legislator is all-powerful—she can determine what policy the majority supports (Black 1948; Downs 1957). The direction and distance between medians—say, between the House as a whole and a conference delegation—provides a measure of bias. Comparing means instead of medians for the units would not substantially change the inferences that we report in this chapter.

Measuring Bias

A challenge in measuring bias is accounting for the differences that would be expected if conference delegations were chosen randomly from the parent chambers, parties, or committees. Conference delegations are often so small that wide differences in liberal-conservative scores between conference delegations and their parent bodies are expected by chance. Remarkably few delegations are so different from their parent bodies that the difference is unlikely to have occurred by chance. As a result, we do not attempt to make claims about the statistical significance of the differences between individual conference delegations and their parent bodies.

We use a method that focuses instead on the aggregate pattern among conferences (see Vander Wielen and Smith 2011). We observe that if the number of conference delegations included in the analysis is large, then it follows that the distribution of differences in liberal-conservative scores between the conference delegation and chamber medians (measured as Conference Delegation Median – Chamber Median) would have a mean of zero if conferees are indeed representative of the parent chamber. That is, if we construct a distribution of differences between conference delegation and chamber medians, the mean of that distribution would be statistically indiscernible from zero if there is no systematic bias in conference delegations. We can then calculate a *p*-value for the null hypothesis that the distribution is centered at zero to determine whether the distribution of conference delegation–chamber differences in medians deviates in a statistically meaningful way from the null expectation of representative delegations. Similar analyses can be used to assess the presence of bias relative to parent parties and committees.

Constructing Conference Delegations

Complex conferences, which we described in chapter 2 as conferences composed of general- and limited-purpose conferees, require careful treatment in evaluating conference delegation bias. We opt to calculate bias for the voting unit implied by House and Senate precedents. In the Senate, a majority of all senators appointed to a conference must sign a conference report for the report to be valid. Thus, for the Senate, we consider all senators appointed to a conference as the unit for which we calculate a median liberal-conservative score that is then compared to the median scores for the parent house and committee. In the House, a majority of conferees who were appointed to consider each provision, as provided in the order appointing them, is required for a report to be valid. In the case of House complex conferences, we use the *sub*conference as the unit for which a median liberal-conservative score is calculated. Thus, when there is a complex House conference with general- and limited-purpose conferees, and therefore multiple subconferences, we use the subconference as the unit of analysis. There can be several subconferences within one conference. For single-committee House conferences, the unit is simply the full conference membership.

The Presence of Bias

Figures 3.2 and 3.3 provide an overview of the median liberal-conservative scores for single-committee conference delegations. We provide similar figures for multi-committee conferences in the appendix, part B (see figures B.1 and B.2); they show very similar patterns. The figures show medians for the two parties, the chamber median, the median for committees

Median

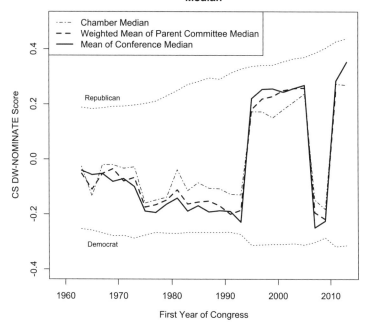

Bias

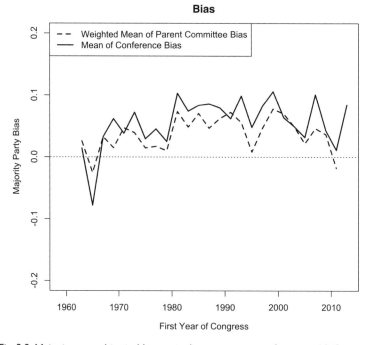

Fig. 3.2. Majority party bias in House single-committee conferences, 1963–2014. (Compiled by the authors from *Calendars of the United States House of Representatives and History of Legislation, Final Edition*, 88th Congress–113th Congress [for the conference membership], Charles Stewart website (http://web.mit.edu/17.251/www/data_page.html) [for standing committee membership], and voteview.org [for CS DW-NOMINATE scores].)

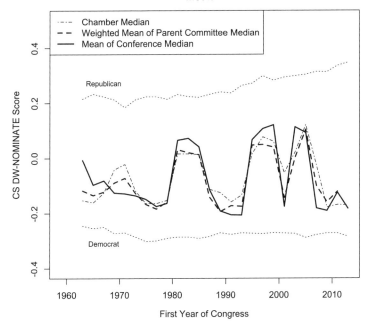

Median

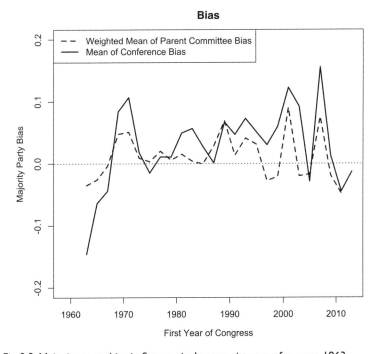

Bias

Fig. 3.3. Majority party bias in Senate single-committee conferences, 1963–2014. (Compiled by the authors from *Calendars of the United States House of Representatives and History of Legislation, Final Edition*, 88th Congress–113th Congress [for the conference membership], Charles Stewart website (http://web.mit.edu/17.251/www/data_page.html) [for standing committee membership], and voteview.org [for CS DW-NOMINATE scores].)

going to conference (a mean weighted by the frequency that a committee goes to conference), and the median for all conference delegations. In the top panel of each figure, it is obvious that the chamber medians move back and forth between the Democratic and Republican side as majority control of each house changes. Committee and conference medians track closely with the chamber medians. From this perspective, the conference bias appears to be small throughout the period since the 1960s.

The bottom panels in the figures zoom in for a closer look at the difference between committee, conference, and chamber medians. The chamber median is set to zero so that we can readily see how committee and conference medians differ from it on average. The differences are small but fairly consistent. On the -1.0 to +1.0 scale, the differences are seldom as much as one-twentieth of the scale. Yet the differences are fairly consistently on the majority party side of the chamber median. Moreover, conference delegations are somewhat more biased than the parent committees. This is consistent with a simple fractional advantage that the majority party enjoys on most committees and most conference delegations. The smaller conference delegations produce a larger fractional advantage than their parent committees. Thus, the system of committees and conferences has yielded a consistent but small majority party advantage.

It is noteworthy that the 1970s ended a period in which the median for conference delegations was sometimes slightly more conservative than committees and the parent chambers. From the 1970s through recent Congresses, the conference delegations track closely with committees and the parent chamber. In fact, the traditional committee/conference practice does not shift the average bias all the way to the majority party median. With polarized parties since the early 1990s, the gap between the chamber medians and committee/conference medians is not large, so there is some reason for a legislator at the majority party median to be less than fully satisfied with the position of the very influential committee and conference medians.

Evidence of Majority Party Bias in the Aggregate Pattern

With the small differences in medians for the parent chambers and average conference delegations, we must investigate whether these differences are larger than we would expect by chance. In tables 3.2 (House) and 3.3 (Senate), we provide data by type of conference delegation. If the preference composition of conference committees is purely a stochastic phenomenon, then we might expect the distribution of conferees to produce a reasonably equitable split between (sub)conferences favoring the majority party and those that do not.

Throughout the period of analysis, a sizable majority of single-committee conference delegations in the House have consistently exhibited the pro-majority-party bias found by Vander Wielen and Smith (2011). The vast majority of single-committee conferences have medians that are located on the majority party side of the chamber median—an average of 73.4 percent per Congress. The percentage of conference delegations by Congress that have medians shifted in the direction of the majority party

TABLE 3.2. Majority party bias of conference committee delegations in the House, 1963–2014

Congress	Majority Party	Single-Committee Conference			Subconference with Both General- and Limited-Purpose Conferees		
		Number	Median on Majority Side		Number	Median on Majority Side	
			Number	Percent		Number	Percent
88	Democratic	86	47	54.65	0		
89	Democratic	147	39	26.53	0		
90	Democratic	136	68	50.00	0		
91	Democratic	153	85	55.56	2	2	100.00
92	Democratic	153	85	55.56	1	0	0.00
93	Democratic	195	129	66.15	4	3	75.00
94	Democratic	164	107	65.24	6	3	50.00
95	Democratic	147	99	67.35	24	20	83.33
96	Democratic	123	76	61.79	43	34	79.07
97	Democratic	67	58	86.57	64	47	73.44
98	Democratic	74	58	78.38	51	34	66.67
99	Democratic	47	36	76.60	123	92	74.80
100	Democratic	46	36	78.26	177	128	72.32
101	Democratic	53	43	81.13	196	117	59.69
102	Democratic	50	40	80.00	145	86	59.31
103	Democratic	46	41	89.13	144	81	56.25
104	Republican	46	34	73.91	79	68	86.08
105	Republican	35	32	91.43	48	43	89.58
106	Republican	44	41	93.18	54	51	94.44
107	Republican	20	18	90.00	71	58	81.69
108	Republican	26	24	92.31	62	53	85.48
109	Republican	17	15	88.24	60	31	51.67
110	Democratic	11	11	100.00	33	24	72.73
111	Democratic	11	8	72.73	13	5	38.46
112	Republican	3	1	33.33	22	22	100.00
113	Republican	2	2	100.00	4	4	100.00

Source: Compiled by the authors from *Calendars of the United States House of Representatives and History of Legislation, Final Edition*, 88th Congress–113th Congress (for the conference membership), and voteview.org (for CS DW-NOMINATE scores)

relative to the chamber median is statistically discernible from the naïve equitable split (at the $p < 0.01$ level).

When limited-purpose conferees became common, starting in the 95th Congress (1977–1978), they exhibited a similarly consistent pro-majority-party bias. The proportion of multi-committee conferences that have medians on the majority party side of the chamber median is an average of 75 percent per Congress for the period since the 95th Congress (1975–2014). Again, this is statistically different than the distribution implied by a random appointment process (at the $p < 0.01$ level).

TABLE 3.3. Majority party bias of conference committee delegations in the Senate, 1963–2014

Congress	Majority Party	Single-Committee Conference			Conference with Both General- and Limited-Purpose Conferees		
		Number	Median on Majority Side		Number	Median on Majority Side	
			Number	Percent		Number	Percent
88	Democratic	91	21	23.08	0	0	
89	Democratic	146	62	42.47	0	0	
90	Democratic	122	49	40.16	16	6	37.50
91	Democratic	157	113	71.97	3	2	66.67
92	Democratic	143	101	70.63	14	5	35.71
93	Democratic	193	113	58.55	9	4	44.44
94	Democratic	162	80	49.38	14	9	64.29
95	Democratic	170	106	62.35	10	6	60.00
96	Democratic	133	81	60.90	11	5	45.45
97	Republican	80	45	56.25	10	7	70.00
98	Republican	87	48	55.17	9	5	55.56
99	Republican	66	42	63.64	12	2	16.67
100	Democratic	63	30	47.62	16	13	81.25
101	Democratic	71	55	77.46	18	12	66.67
102	Democratic	76	51	67.11	12	7	58.33
103	Democratic	67	54	80.60	4	2	50.00
104	Republican	56	29	51.79	9	4	44.44
105	Republican	44	28	63.64	7	5	71.43
106	Republican	51	34	66.67	7	5	71.43
107	Democratic	36	33	91.67	2	2	100.00
108	Republican	41	27	65.85	4	2	50.00
109	Republican	27	12	44.44	6	2	33.33
110	Democratic	20	20	100.00	1	1	100.00
111	Democratic	16	11	68.75	2	2	100.00
112	Democratic	6	2	33.33	1	0	0.00
113	Republican	4	3	75.00	0	0	

Source: Compiled by the authors from *Calendars of the United States House of Representatives and History of Legislation, Final Edition*, 88th Congress–113th Congress (for the conference membership), and voteview.org (for CS DW-NOMINATE scores)

A pro-majority-party bias also is common in the Senate (see table 3.3), although the frequency of bias is significantly smaller than that observed in the House. On average, 61.1 percent of single-committee conferences have medians situated on the majority party side of the chamber median per Congress, and 57.5 percent of multi-committee conferences likewise exhibit pro-majority-party bias. The percent of single-committee conferences exhibiting a pro-majority bias is statistically significant (at the p < 0.01 level). The finding that the Senate exhibits bias that is more subdued than in the House also parallels the findings of Vander Wielen and Smith (2011), who argue that differences in the institutions governing the appointment of conferees across the chambers place greater constraints on party leaders in their pursuit of partisan goals.

The House results point to a marked increase in the pro-majority-party bias over time. In the period where conference committees dominated post-passage politics (the 88th–94th Congresses), an average of 53.4 percent of single-committee conferences had their medians shifted toward the majority party median—barely more than half. However, this proportion increased during periods with more polarized parties: to an average of 77.7 percent in the 95th–103rd Congresses (1977–1994) and to an average of 83.5 percent after the 104th Congress. For multi-committee conferences, an average of 69.4 percent had their medians located on the majority party side of the parent chamber median between the 95th and 103rd Congresses, but it increased to an average of 80 percent after the 104th Congress. The Senate also shows a similar pattern of increasing pro-majority-party bias, which is unsurprising considering that it experienced similar trends in partisanship over time.

General- versus Limited-Purpose Conferees

We have no theory or practical expectations about the relative bias in general-purpose versus limited-purpose subconferences of the same conference. As a general rule, we would expect the two subconferences to have somewhat different interests, but for many multi-committee bills there is no reason to expect that one type of subconference will exhibit a systematically stronger majority party bias than another. Nonetheless, the difference between the two types is worth a quick look. We report the relevant data and tests in tables 3.4 and 3.5. Note that these tables report subconference-level statistics on the pro-majority-party bias of limited-purpose conferees relative to general-purpose conferees and all voting members of the subconference.

The differences between general- and limited-purpose delegations are noteworthy. On average, 68.9 percent of limited-purpose delegation medians in the House are more closely situated to the majority party median than their general-purpose counterparts (the difference is statistically significant at the $p < 0.01$ level). In addition, we similarly find that an average of 63.2 percent of medians for limited-purpose conferees in the House exhibit pro-majority-party bias relative to all members with voting rights on the subconference (i.e., limited- and general-purpose conferees on the subconference combined). This, too, is a percentage that is statistically significant ($p < 0.01$), despite being a more rigorous test of bias.[2] The t-statistics further indicate that the policy distances between limited-purpose conferees and both general-purpose conferees and all members with voting

TABLE 3.4. Comparison of bias in general- and limited-purpose subconferences in House multi-committee conferences, 1971–2014

Congress	Majority Party	Number of Limited-Purpose Subconference	Median on Majority Side of General-Purpose Subconference Median		Median on Majority Side of All Subconference Median	
			Number	Percent	Number	Percent
92	Democratic	1	1	100.00	1	100.00
93	Democratic	3	3	100.00	1	33.33
94	Democratic	1	1	100.00	1	100.00
95	Democratic	15	10	66.67	10	66.67
96	Democratic	33	20	60.61	19	57.58
97	Democratic	60	38	63.33	38	63.33
98	Democratic	49	24	48.98	24	48.98
99	Democratic	122	85	69.67	76	62.30
100	Democratic	175	102	58.29	101	57.71
101	Democratic	192	107	55.73	98	51.04
102	Democratic	144	70	48.61	67	46.53
103	Democratic	141	50	35.46	75	53.19
104	Republican	78	48	61.54	38	48.72
105	Republican	48	28	58.33	28	58.33
106	Republican	53	33	62.26	30	56.60
107	Republican	71	42	59.15	44	61.97
108	Republican	59	42	71.19	39	66.10
109	Republican	58	44	75.86	42	72.41
110	Democratic	33	26	78.79	25	75.76
111	Democratic	13	9	69.23	9	69.23
112	Republican	22	16	72.73	9	40.91
113	Republican	3	3	100.00	3	100.00

Source: Compiled by the authors from *Calendars of the United States House of Representatives and History of Legislation, Final Edition*, 88th Congress–113th Congress (for the conference membership), and voteview.org (for CS DW-NOMINATE scores)

rights on the subconference are, in many Congresses, greater than would be expected by chance. Nevertheless, the frequency of pro-majority bias is considerably smaller than the substantial pro-majority-party bias that we see for conferences relative to the parent chambers. And it goes without saying that the magnitude of this bias (along the liberal-conservative scale) is significantly smaller as well.

The relationship between limited- and general-purpose conferees observed in the House does not extend to the Senate. In fact, on average, only a slim majority of the medians for limited-purpose conferees favor the majority party relative to the medians of general-purpose conferees (an average of 51.9 percent), which fails to achieve statistical significance. And, on average, only about 41.9 percent of limited-purpose medians are located

TABLE 3.5. Comparison of bias in general- and limited-purpose subconferences in Senate multi-committee conferences, 1973–2014

Congress	Majority Party	Number of Limited-Purpose Subconference	Median on Majority Side of General-Purpose Subconference Median		Median on Majority Side of All Conference Median	
			Number	Percent	Number	Percent
93	Democratic	2	2	100.00	0	0.00
94	Democratic	1	0	0.00	0	0.00
95	Democratic	7	3	42.86	2	28.57
96	Democratic	18	6	33.33	6	33.33
97	Republican	24	12	50.00	13	54.17
98	Republican	14	10	71.43	6	42.86
99	Republican	28	13	46.43	14	50.00
100	Democratic	35	17	48.57	12	34.29
101	Democratic	24	15	62.50	10	41.67
102	Democratic	15	8	53.33	8	53.33
103	Democratic	1	0	0.00	0	0.00
104	Republican	14	8	57.14	10	71.43
105	Republican	17	9	52.94	7	41.18
106	Republican	8	6	75.00	5	62.50
107	Democratic	2	2	100.00	2	100.00
108	Republican	1	1	100.00	1	100.00
109	Republican	5	2	40.00	2	40.00
110	Democratic	3	0	0.00	0	0.00
111	Democratic	0				
112	Democratic	0				
113	Republican	0				

Source: Compiled by the authors from *Calendars of the United States House of Representatives and History of Legislation, Final Edition*, 88th Congress–113th Congress (for the conference membership), and voteview. org (for CS DW-NOMINATE scores).

on the majority party side of the median for the entire subconference—a percentage that, likewise, fails to achieve statistical significance. Thus, in the Senate, we no longer observe pro-majority bias for limited-purpose conferees relative to general-purpose conferees.

The Correlates of Conference Bias

To this point, we have found differences in the patterns of conference committee bias across the chambers that fit our expectations. The House exhibits more bias and has experienced more systematic changes in bias related to the waves of change in post-passage politics that have occurred in the past half century. Before leaving our consideration of partisan bias, we want to explore the factors responsible for the considerable variation we observe across conferences in terms of the direction and size of bias. Even in the Congresses for which we found a large number of pro-majority-party conference delegation medians relative to the chamber median, we often observe a nontrivial percentage of delegations that showed a bias on the minority party side of the chamber median, at least by some modest amount. This variation is visible in figure 3.4, which provides the distribution of conference delegation bias over the entire period we are examining.

We model the correlates of bias in conference delegations using the distance between the voting conferees' median and the chamber median on the liberal-conservative scale as our dependent variable. As before, this measure is operationalized in a way that presents positive values for pro-majority-party bias and negative values for pro-minority-party bias. We fit models with the House and Senate data both separated and pooled.

Our discussion directs our attention to several sets of factors that may shape the nature of conference delegation bias. Three types of factors are of particular interest: the fractional advantage enjoyed by the majority party on committees and conferences, the partisan interest in committees and conferences, and the nature of interparty conflict. Each of these factors warrants brief discussion.

The Fractional Advantage

We have observed that translating party ratios from the parent chamber to committees and conference delegations creates an opportunity for the majority party to "round up" and give itself small fractional advantages when determining the number of seats to be allocated to each party on a

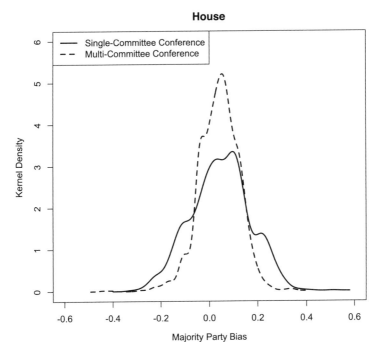

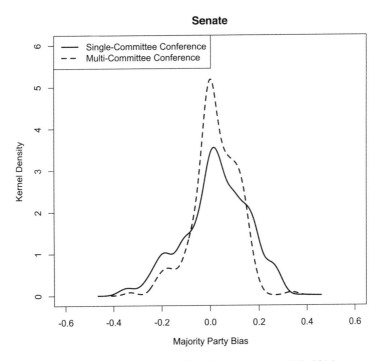

Fig. 3.4. Distribution of majority party bias in conferences, 1963–2014

standing committee or conference delegation. A small seat advantage to the majority party is a common occurrence. This advantage is deliberately extended for some House committees. The advantage comes in the form of an additional one or two seats that boosts the majority representation slightly above the chamber proportion. For complex conferences, which are those with subconferences composed of general- and limited-purpose conferees, the advantage can be additive across the two groups that comprise a particular subconference.[3]

An additional possibility, which we explore here, is that the advantage gained by the majority party is larger when a conference delegation is small and rounding up can make the largest difference. However, an argument can be made that enlarging conference delegations gives the majority party an opportunity to add friendly members more freely. Majority leaders, as the argument goes, may choose to expand delegations for the purpose of reaching deeper into committees while respecting the seniority norm, which ultimately generates greater opportunity for biasing the delegations more in favor of the majority party (Lazarus and Monroe 2007).

Preliminary evidence supports the view that smaller delegations favor the majority party, at least on average. As table 3.6 shows, the correlations are very small, but delegation size is related to pro-majority-party bias. The relationship is strongest in the most recent period since the Republican takeover after the 1994 elections, where the correlation between conference size and pro-majority bias is -0.2. Therefore, we include a measure of delegation size in our models.

TABLE 3.6. Correlation between conference size and conference bias

| | | Single-Committee Conferences | Multi-Committee Conferences | |
			General-Purpose	Limited-Purpose
House	88–93	0.17		
	94–103	−0.03	−0.15	−0.03
	104–113	−0.20	−0.03	−0.15
	All	0.10	−0.10	−0.07
Senate	88–93	0.10		
	94–103	−0.12	−0.17	0.16
	104–113	−0.32	−0.42	−0.09
	All	−0.02	−0.14	0.08

Source: Compiled by the authors from *Calendars of the United States House of Representatives and History of Legislation, Final Edition*, 88th Congress–113th Congress (for the conference membership), and voteview.org (for CS DW-NOMINATE scores).

Committee Type

Political scientists have long realized that standing committees vary widely in their relevance to party interests (Cox and McCubbins 2007; Fenno 1973; Maltzman 1997; Deering and Smith 1997). Fiscal policy committees (i.e., Appropriations, Budget, Finance, Ways and Means) are usually central to the differences between the two parties, engage in policy making that matters to nearly all members, and generate legislation that produces partisan divisions on the floor. These committees are sometimes labeled "prestige" committees because of the special status that is associated with membership on them. Other committees (i.e., Energy, Education, Banking, Judiciary), sometimes called "policy" committees, also are regularly relevant to party interests. Prestige and policy committees are sometimes distinguished from "constituency" committees that have jurisdiction over matters of less general interest, report legislation that does not create partisan divisions, and seldom is of major interest to party leaders.

These distinctions lead to the testable proposition that prestige and policy committees attract the interest of party leaders and motivate the appointment of extra majority party members to their committees and conference delegations. With respect to standing committees of the 114th Congress (2015–2016), for example, House Republicans held 56.6 percent of House seats, but they gave themselves over 61 percent of the seats on Budget and on Ways and Means (and 69 percent on Rules), while giving themselves 58 percent of the seats on policy and constituency committees. To be sure, these are small differences, but they give the majority party a little breathing room to account for absences and wayward members.

On conference delegations, we might expect that party leaders, and their party colleagues who are placing demands on them, care more about outcomes in conferences with the greatest implications for the party, which are those associated with the prestige and, to a lesser degree, the policy committees. At times, this may involve ensuring that the balance of views on the conference delegation favor the party position. If the same considerations affect the appointment of standing committees, then simply appointing a cross-section of committee members to conferences may produce the desired results in conferences. Thus, we might not expect bias among conferees beyond what we observe in the parent committees. We model the effect of committee type on conference bias below, controlling for the bias in parent committees.

Party Strategies

We have emphasized that intensifying interparty competition and polarizing parties have altered the context of post-passage politics in fundamental ways. Two waves of change have emerged over the last generation. The first wave produced a "Democratic era" of enlarged and multi-committee conferences. The second wave, largely a "Republican era," involved some reduction in delegation sizes, more partisan control of conferences, and eventually the demise of conferencing. The direct implication of these changes is rising pro-majority bias in conference delegations over the two waves of change. We already have seen the evidence for this and account for the eras in the models we estimate.

It is tempting to more directly estimate the effects of interparty competition and polarization on conference delegation bias by including variables for both factors in models of individual delegation bias. In fact, it is so tempting that we try it. However, our expectation is that these variables will not perform well. The only way we can measure these concepts is to give all delegations within a chamber and Congress the same competition and polarization values. With our data (just twenty-two Congresses), it is very difficult to find significant Congress-to-Congress effects for those measures.

House-Senate Differences

The House and Senate are expected to differ with respect to conference bias. The opportunities for party influence are more direct in the House than in the Senate. In the House, the opportunity for majority party influence is particularly pronounced because the Speaker, under House Rule I, Clause 11, is empowered to appoint conferees without the approval of the House. In contrast, before 2013, the Senate motions to go to conference and to authorize the chair to appoint conferees were divisible and debatable, which gave the minority multiple opportunities to obstruct a conference. Since 2013, the motion to appoint conferees is combined with the motion to go to conference, but it can still be filibustered. Because the Senate majority party cannot expect minority party cooperation if it reserves extra conference appointments for itself or appoints members who are drastically unrepresentative of the chamber, the majority party bias introduced in appointing conferees is likely to be limited. As a general rule, then, the majority party bias in conference appointments is likely to be smaller in the Senate than the House.[4]

Multivariate Estimates

The bivariate relationships we have reviewed may be misleading—after all, some of the factors may be related to each other and not have significant independent effects on majority party bias. To check this, we report the results for estimates of multivariate linear models of majority bias in table 3.7. Models are estimated separately for Senate conferences, House single-committee conferences, and House multi-committee conferences. We also present the results of a model that pools the House and Senate data. The full results are reported in tables B-1 and B-2 in the appendix, part B; we identify only the relationships that are statistically significant in this table. The first three columns in the table report the results for the two types of House conferences (single-committee conferences and subconferences from multi-committee conferences) and Senate conferences. The fourth column, which pools all conferences and House subconferences, allows us to estimate the effect of the chamber, controlling for other variables.

The estimates confirm these expectations about majority party bias in conference delegations:

- Senate conference delegation bias is smaller than House conference delegation bias;
- for House multi-committee subconferences and Senate conferences, the size of the delegation is inversely related to bias (fractional advantage is confirmed);
- conference delegation bias is positively related to the parent committee's bias;
- conference delegations on important bills show more bias than delegations on unimportant bills, although the distinction does not apply to multi-committee subconference delegations because there are few unimportant bills with complex conferences; and
- majority party bias increased in multi-committee subconferences in the House in recent eras.

The hypotheses about the three important policy domains—appropriations, budget, taxes—are largely unconfirmed. For the House conferences, this outcome is primarily due to the inclusion of variables for bill importance in the equations, which accounts for most of the variance that would be explained by the variables for the three domains (data not shown). For the tax domain, the negative and statistically significant coefficient in the Senate model is contrary to our expectations.

TABLE 3.7. Multivariate linear model for conference bias

	House		Senate Conference	Pooled
	Single-Committee Conference	Multi-Committee Conference		
Chamber				
- House (omitted)				
- Senate	n.a.	n.a.	n.a.	-
Conference size		-	-	-
General-purpose parent committee bias	+	+	+	+
Limited-purpose parent committee bias	n.a.	+	n.a.	n.a.
General-purpose parent committee type				
- Constituency committee (omitted)				
- Policy committee	+	+	+	+
- Prestige committee		+	-	-
Limited-purpose parent committee type				
- Constituency committee (omitted)				
- Policy committee	n.a.	(+)	n.a.	n.a.
- Prestige committee				
Important bill				
- Least important (omitted)				
- Somewhat important	+			+
- Highly important	+			
Partisan bill				
- No roll call vote (omitted)				
- Roll call but no party vote		-	-	
- Party vote	+			+
Policy domain				
- Appropriations				
- Budget				+
- Tax			-	-
- Others (omitted)				
Congress-level partisan environment				-
- Interparty distance	+	-		
- Majority party homogeneity	(-)	+		
- Majority party size	-	(-)	-	-
Period				
- First wave (95th-103rd)		+		+
- Second wave (104th-112th)		+		+
Constant		+	+	+
N	1,559	984	1,830	4,408
F-statistic	50.19*	24.51*	121.12*	146.06*
R²	0.34	0.33	0.52	0.36

Note: Unit of analysis is the voting unit of each chamber's conference delegations; dependent variable is the conference bias toward the majority party; entries are statistically significant relationships ($p < 0.05$), with positive (+) and negative (-) directions ($p < 0.1$ in parenthesis); whenever categorical variables are used, the omitted baseline category is noted; independent variables that are not included in the model are denoted as n.a. (not applicable).

The results for the variables capturing partisan effects are mixed. The presence of a party vote on final passage in the House is related to majority party bias only for single-committee conferences in the House. The Congress-level measures of partisan environment are not expected to predict bias well, and the variables intended to capture the distribution of preferences within and across the parties (i.e., *Inter-party distance* and *Majority party homogeneity*) show largely null or opposite effects. The liberal or conservative makeup of conference delegations is clearly related to party polarization, as shown in figures 3.2 and 3.3 above, but we find little evidence of bias beyond the polarization that occurs via the parent parties and committees. However, we find evidence consistent with the notion that pro-majority bias in conference is linked to partisan competition. Specifically, as majority party size increases, and thus party competition wanes, we see a corresponding decrease in pro-majority bias. Given that party interests become more central to members' decision-making calculus under conditions of intense party competition, and thus party leaders take a more active role throughout the legislative process (including the post-passage stage), these findings confirm our expectations.

The period effects are significant only for multi-committee House subconferences. We have seen that majority party bias was greater after the two waves of change in post-passage politics. That is not apparent in these estimates because we have controlled for many of the committee and party factors that changed with the two waves—conference sizes, parent committee bias, and party polarization. When these variables are excluded, the period effects are positive and significant (results not shown here).

Conclusion

We have discovered a general pattern in majority party bias in conferences. It is a bias baked into the committee and party foundations of conference membership. Significant sources of conference delegation bias are the bias of the parent committees, rounding up to determine majority party numbers on delegations, and the additive effect of rounding up when appointing general- and limited-purpose conferees for subconferences on important measures. The accumulation of small advantages usually gives the majority party a larger comfort zone on conference delegations than its chamber representation alone would suggest. We confirm the proposition that conference delegations have preferences more closely aligned with the majority party than would be expected by chance alone.

Moreover, we have observed that the patterns are predicted by the changing political environment of congressional policy making. More intense partisan competition and deeper party polarization are associated with greater pro-majority-party bias in conferences. While conferences themselves fell victim to those forces, with majority parties turning to other post-passage strategies across successive waves of change, the conferences that remained exhibited more bias. In recent Congresses, of course, conferences virtually disappeared, and non-conference processes fully controlled by party leaders took over.

Finally, it bears special emphasis that the institutional context matters. We found that the pro-majority-party bias in conference delegations became stronger in the House than in the Senate. The Senate minority's ability to check the majority's moves to appoint conferees, and perhaps even its ability to filibuster conference reports, served to temper the partisan bias that could be structured into Senate conference delegations and muted the effects that party competition and polarization might have had on Senate delegations.

FOUR

Five Stories on the Collapse
of Conferencing

As we have seen, the legislative process is malleable. The Constitution requires that the House and Senate pass legislation in identical form, but is silent on how the House and Senate prepare legislation for approval. The House and Senate have evolved flexible processes for doing this—sending legislation to a conference committee, exchanging amendments, or just accepting the work of the other house—but these methods can be mixed and matched at the will of chamber majorities. Moreover, rules that govern what can be done in conference—which, of course, do not have constitutional or legal force—can be changed, waived, or ignored.

We have argued that the structure of the legislative process reflects inherited institutional arrangements, the competitiveness of the parties, and the distribution of policy preferences between the parties. Basic institutions are seldom changed, although the budget process reshaped the process for making fiscal policy decisions in important ways. Competition between the parties for control of the institutions of government, particularly in a long period of narrow majorities and frequent changes in party control, can create incentives for a more party-oriented process, a less committee-dominated process, and a process geared more to electoral considerations than policy considerations. And the homogeneity of the majority party and the distance between the parties can influence how assertive party leaders are in directing the process of writing and passing legislation.

In this chapter, we dig deeper by exploring the post-passage politics of five major policy domains. We begin with fiscal policy legislation: appropriations, tax, and budget measures. We then turn to defense authorization and agricultural/food stamp bills. Three themes emerge from this exploration.

First, the fiscal policy domain, which was central to both changes in institutional arrangements and party conflict, plays an exceptionally large role in the pattern observed in previous chapters. Budget, spending, and tax bills were combined in a wide variety of ways that changed the formal procedures by which some of the most important legislating was done, reshaping post-passage politics in significant ways.

Second, omnibus legislating—fewer but larger measures—did more than reduce the number of measures going to conference. If omnibus legislating is all there is to it, then we would predict that the increasing complexity of enacted measures would increase the proportion of measures passed by the House and Senate going to conference. After all, judging by mid-twentieth century practice, conferences are expected for large, complex bills that almost always involve dozens of differences between House and Senate versions. However, that is not what we observe. The proportion of bills passed that are resolved in conference committees has plummeted, too. The politics that generate fewer but larger legislative measures also involves delays, innovations in the process of devising legislation and building House and Senate coalitions, and procedural novelties that reduced the use of conference committees to complete the drafting of legislation.

Third, and most important, the various policy domains exhibit substantial differences in post-passage politics. As we will see, conference committees have continued to be central to legislative action on the major defense and agricultural bills while conference committees have proven less common and less important to interchamber agreements on fiscal policy. The differences in post-passage politics reflect differences in the larger institutional and partisan environment across the policy domains. They lead us to exercise caution in generalizing about the changes in post-passage legislating.

The Institutional and Partisan Context

Our theme has been that the evolving character of post-passage politics is a by-product of changes in the larger environment of congressional politics. The evolving political context of post-passage resolution processes was detailed in chapter 1. Here, we return to the inherited institutions, interparty competition, and party polarization with closer attention to their implications for the five legislative domains. Even with the powerful forces of intensified partisanship in electoral and policy arenas that have reached into nearly all corners of congressional policy making, there remain important variations in how Democrats and Republicans relate to each other, particularly in the committee setting, that can influence the nature of post-passage decision making. A quick review of the forces discussed in chapter 1 will set up our expectations for variation in post-passage experiences for House and Senate committees across these policy domains.

Institutional Context

In chapter 1, we emphasized how the strongly committee-oriented decision-making processes internal to the House and Senate shaped an equally committee-oriented process for resolving House-Senate differences. In any Congress of the mid-twentieth century, members of the standing committees inherited a long-standing way of doing things imposed by committee chairs who had acquired their positions through seniority. The senior members of committees, with few exceptions, constituted conference delegations for their chambers whenever a bill went to conference.

This way of doing things was challenged in the late 1960s. Factionalism among Democrats, particularly House Democrats, led to important committee reforms. In the early 1970s, liberals seeking to reduce the influence of conservative Democrats, who held a disproportionate share of committee chairmanships in the 1960s, successfully increased the importance of subcommittees and increased the Speaker's options in referring legislation to committees. In addition, the liberals in the House spearheaded the adoption of a rule that urged the Speaker to appoint the major proponents of key provisions to conference delegations so that their interests would have a voice in conference. The expectation we discussed in chapter 1 and subsequently reported on in chapter 3 was that representation on House conference delegations would be broader and more representative of the Democratic caucus following these reforms.

Nearly simultaneously with the committee reforms, the House created a new budget process in 1974. The Budget Act provided for two new committees, the House and Senate Budget Committees. The budget committees write the budget resolutions and package reconciliation legislation from various committees ordered to adjust the programs under their jurisdiction. Starting in 1980, reconciliation bills, which must be authorized by a budget resolution, began to be considered before the traditional appropriations, authorization, and tax legislation was passed. In fact, the 1974 budget process was intended to give more emphasis to the aggregate effects of spending and tax decisions and to more explicitly connect them to an overall budget. It has worked out that way, and with important consequences. Aggregate budget decisions focused attention on the size and role of government, which emerged as a central difference between the parties. The once decentralized, committee-by-committee, bill-by-bill legislating was replaced by legislating concentrated in a few bills, constructed by the budget committees in some cases, and always supervised by top party leaders.

Party Competition

As we noted in chapter 1, congressional parties entered a period of intense competition for majority control of Congress in the 1980s (see Gamm and Smith forthcoming). Parties invested more in public relations, messaging, credit claiming, and blame attribution, and few major issues were approached without regard to their electoral consequences. Through the expansion of public relations staffs, the use of new technologies, and the appointment of legislators to devise "war room" strategies and daily messages, parties became better equipped to spread the partisan enterprise to more and more issues. These partisan, electorally-oriented activities, and the central role that leaders play in the process, spill into post-passage politics, particularly on salient legislation.

Party Polarization

In chapter 1, we observed how much more polarized the two parties became in their overall voting records in the period since the 1970s. It is not surprising that the polarization exhibited in aggregate floor voting also appears in the party delegations on the five committees with immediate jurisdiction over the policy domains considered in this chapter. Figure 4.1 shows the difference in the parties' mean Common Space DW-NOMINATE scores, the same scores described in chapters 1 and 3, for the members of the five House and Senate committees. In the 1960s, the distance between the parties varied widely from committee to committee in both houses. Since the early 1970s, as the distance between the parties began to grow overall, the committees became more similar. In a manner that parallels the frequency of party voting by domain in the House (see figure 4.2), the distance between the parties tends to be greatest for the budget and tax committees. In fact, the interparty distance has been greatest for those two committees in both houses in recent Congresses. In the House, Agriculture, Appropriations, and Armed Services tend to show

House

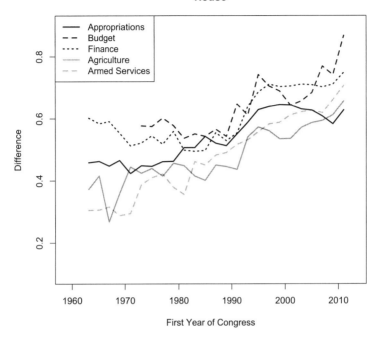

First Year of Congress

Senate

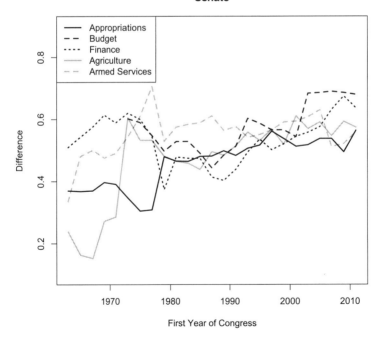

First Year of Congress

Fig. 4.1. Difference in liberal-conservative scores, by committee, 1963–2012. (Compiled by the authors from Charles Stewart website (http://web.mit. edu/17.251/www/data_page.html) [for standing committee membership] and voteview.org [for CS DW-NOMINATE scores].)

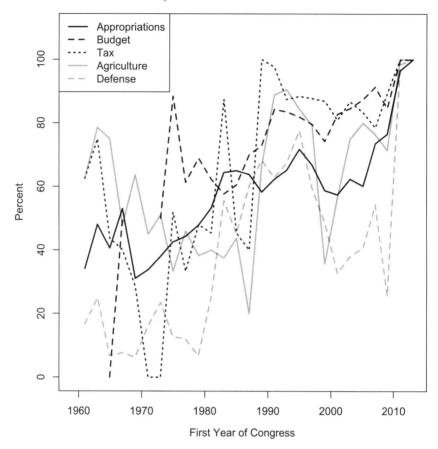

Fig. 4.2. Percentage of votes that were party votes, House final passage, by policy domain, 1963–2014. (Compiled by the authors from Political Institutions and Public Choice Roll-Call Database.)

smaller distances between the parties than either the Budget or Ways and Means committees. In the Senate, with much smaller committees, differences among committees are not so great or consistent.

A Matching Analysis

One simple interpretation of our arguments is that the post-passage processes were likely to be different, even for similar legislation, in the three periods described in previous chapters. It is possible, even likely, the nature of the bills reaching the post-passage stage changed in ways that affected the post-passage method, particularly between the second and third periods as congressional policy making became more intensely partisan. For example, partisan conflict may have reduced the number of important, complex bills and so reduced the relative number of conference committees. If so, then it also is possible that the decline in the use of conference evolved because of changes in the structure of the legislative agenda and only indirectly because of changes in the partisan context.

Matching analysis (Ho et al. 2007) is designed to help us sort out these complications. By matching bills from different eras in key characteristics other than partisan conflict to analytically make the legislative agendas in the pre-1994 and post-1994 eras look similar, we can then compare post-passage methods with some confidence that the matching variables are not causing all of the difference. We report such an analysis in the appendix, part C, by accounting for differences among bills in importance, policy domain, and fiscal/non-fiscal content. The bottom line is that the decline in the use of conferences remains, and this decline is statistically significant, even after the matching exercise is done.

Some Expectations

We can match in a more complete and concrete way by examining changes in post-passage processes for bills that *recur* in many Congresses over the five-and-a-half decades we have studied. These bills match on issue and committee of origin, and often share the same name. We examine five sets of these bills—a range of bills that include a large proportion of important measures and of measures that once went to conference. Differences in their centrality to the changes in partisan conflict should be related to differences in the patterns of change in post-passage processes that we observe. They are.

The differences in institutional and partisan environments across policy domains and committees imply that we should find greater change in the decision-making processes in the fiscal policy domains than in the agriculture and defense policy domains. All policy domains may have been affected by intensified partisan competition and sharper partisan polarization, but agriculture and defense legislation has been associated with *relatively* less partisanship than the fiscal policy domains. In addition, and often as a product of partisan strategies, the budget process and partisan battles have altered the legislative vehicles for fiscal policy legislation more than the most important agriculture and defense authorization bills.

These differences in decision-making processes should be reflected in the way in which the House and Senate resolve their differences. The comparatively weaker partisan pressures, less direct intervention by central party leaders, and less influence over fiscal issues should give agriculture and armed services committee members more leeway to use traditional conferences to finalize the details of legislation within their jurisdiction. To test this expectation, we consider major bills in each of the five policy domains, starting with appropriations, budget, and taxes, and then turning to agriculture and defense authorizations.

Appropriations Bills

Appropriations bills, which give federal agencies the authority to spend funds from the federal treasury, constituted a large and regular part of the congressional agenda for decades. Over the last century, the number of regular appropriations bills has varied from 10 to 15 per year. In the middle decades of the twentieth century, about a fifth of all conferences were created to resolve House-Senate differences on regular appropriations bills. Less regular but common appropriations bills—supplemental appropriations to deal with additional spending demands, continuing resolutions to allow spending while full-year appropriations bills await action, and even rescission bills to cut previously approved spending—add to the number of appropriations measures, which sometimes totaled more than three dozen in a Congress, most of which were associated with conference committees.

The major role of appropriations in congressional policy making is suggested by figure 4.3, which shows the proportion of all enacted legislation (i.e., public laws) that went through conference within the five policy domains considered in this chapter. Appropriations measures clearly dominate. Before the 1990s, appropriations measures were regularly responsible for 20–30 percent of the conferences. As the number of conferences in other policy domains declined in the 1990s and thereafter, appropriations became a larger share of the total. Since 1990, about half of all conferences have been for appropriations measures.

As a general rule, the House and Senate appropriations committees have created a subcommittee for each regular appropriations bill. New governmental functions, and the associated growth in the number and size of executive departments and agencies, led the appropriations committees to restructure subcommittees and bills from time to time. A change in party control often was the convenient time to make such adjustments. The regular bills and subcommittees numbered 12 in 1967. When a 13th bill was added, the appropriations committees of both houses maintained,

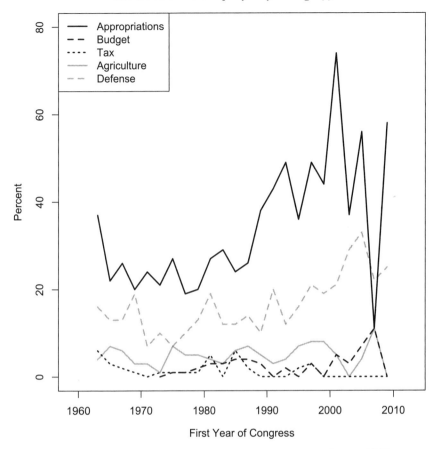

Fig. 4.3. Percent of public laws going to conference, by policy domain, 1963–2010. (Compiled by the authors from Policy Agenda Project.)

with brief exceptions, 13 subcommittees and regular bills through 2004. A restructuring reduced the number of subcommittees to 10 House and 12 Senate subcommittees in 2005, and another set of changes produced 12 subcommittees and bills in 2007. The number has remained at 12 since then (Saturno and Tollestrup 2015). If the regular appropriations bills successfully covered all of Congress's appropriations activity in a Congress, as many as 24 (or, earlier, 26) conferences would be held.

For appropriations legislation, as much as in any domain of congressional policy making in the mid-twentieth century, legislators had vested interests in a committee-oriented conference process. The practice of assigning one regular appropriations bill to each subcommittee mattered for post-passage politics. As intended, this practice gave a group of appropriations committee members in each chamber a leading role in determining the details of one bill. Conference committees provided a standard way for the senior members of each subcommittee to influence the final content of bills that originated in their subcommittees. Over the years, the paired leaders of the House and Senate appropriations committees and subcommittees (and staff) developed strong relationships that, in most cases, facilitated the resolution of interchamber differences. These legislators had a strong incentive to preserve their subcommittees' special roles in the post-passage process.

Spending on federal domestic and defense programs is an issue that has long pitted the two parties against each other. The partisan pattern usually has been that Democrats have favored higher levels of spending for domestic programs and Republicans have favored more for defense programs.

A Brief History

The 1960s were an extension of the years of "normalcy" in congressional appropriations politics that extended from the 1920s to 1969. Regular appropriations bills, originating in the subcommittees of the House Appropriations Committee, passed both houses most of the time and House-Senate differences were resolved in conference committees. A supplemental appropriation was enacted from time to time to provide funding for purposes that had not been anticipated at the time regular bills were initiated, and even these special bills were usually finalized in conference.

At times, divided control of the House, Senate, and presidency produced temporary gridlock and failure to pass regular appropriations bills on schedule. During the Nixon administration (1969–74), with a Republican in the White House and Democrats in firm control of both houses of Congress, presidential vetoes of appropriations bills forced a showdown over appropriations. In turn, Congress adopted several continuing resolutions to temporarily fund government programs and supplemental appropriations to back up continuing resolutions to meet the demands on programs.

"Non-regular" bills, particularly supplemental appropriations, were common before the Nixon years, but, as figure 4.4 shows, Congress resorted to them much more frequently in the Nixon era (91st–93rd Congresses). During this period, most continuing resolutions were passed on an emergency basis, simply continued funding at past levels, and did not involve the use of formal post-passage methods. As figure 4.5 shows, this increased the number of appropriations bills simply approved by the Sen-

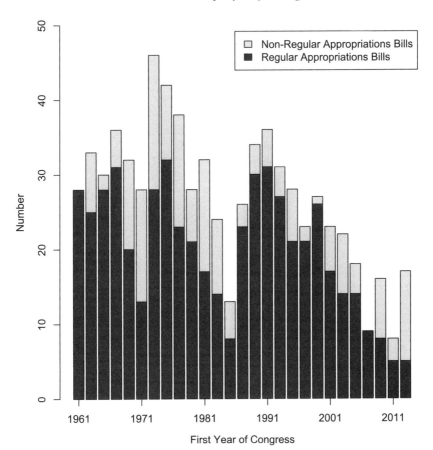

Fig. 4.4. Number of appropriations bills enacted, by type of bill, 1961–2014. (Compiled by the authors from *CQ Almanac*.)

ate without a formal post-passage process required. Past supplemental appropriations typically went to conference, as did all regular appropriations bills that were passed by both houses. After the battles with Nixon, Democratic Congresses returned to passing most regular appropriations bills with conferences.

In the 1980s, sharp conflict over fiscal policy returned in the Republican Reagan administration, when divided party control led to stalemates over appropriations. In the 98th–100th Congresses (1983–1988), disagreements over spending levels and some substantive issues led to full-year continuing resolutions for many regular appropriations bills. One such continuing resolution covered all appropriations bills in 1986, when Democrats

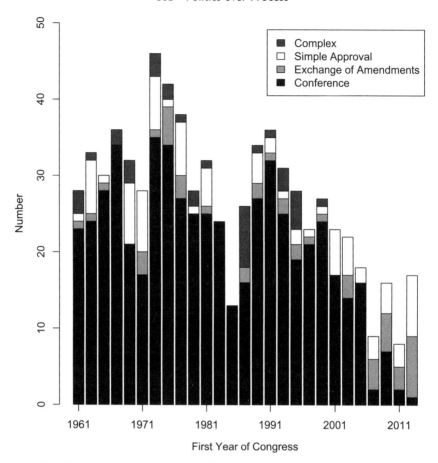

Fig. 4.5. Number of appropriations bills enacted, by House-Senate reconciliation method, 1961–2014. (Compiled by the authors from *CQ Almanac*.)

controlled the House, Republicans controlled the Senate, and President Reagan was in the second year of his second term.

Congress returned to more regular appropriations bills and conferences in Reagan's last year in office (1988), when budget agreements (see below) called a truce to annual battles over appropriations for a few years. This continued during the administration of Republican president George H. W. Bush (1989–992, 101st–102nd Congresses) and the first Congress of Democratic president Bill Clinton (1993–94).

In the period since the mid-1990s, we have witnessed the deterioration of the traditional appropriations process. Rather than pass 12 or 13 regular appropriations bills initiated by appropriations subcommittees and resolved in a similar number of conference committees, fiscal policy making has centered in congressional parties and the president. Partisan and sometimes factional differences over spending, taxes, debt limits, and other issues have frequently stalled regular bills or, particularly in the Senate where the minority can often block action by filibuster, cut short any serious effort to pass regular bills. A common outcome is a large, omnibus appropriations measure passed to reflect a last-minute deal arranged by top leaders. An omnibus bill, even when taken to conference, greatly reduces the number of conferences and usually reduces the number of legislators in the negotiations.

The 2013 fight over Fiscal 2014 appropriations illustrates the radical changes that occurred in the appropriations process. At the start of the fiscal year on October 1, 2013, none of the 12 regular bills had passed. The House committee had reported all but one of the regular bills, but the House had passed only four of them. The Senate committee had approved all but one of them, but only one was debated on the floor and it was set aside after Republicans successfully blocked cloture on the bill. Contributing to the breakdown of the process was the inability of the two houses to agree on a budget resolution that would set spending targets and guide appropriations decisions. Leaders of the two houses made little serious effort to pass a continuing resolution, which led to a 16-day shutdown of many government agencies. The House had passed three continuing resolutions, but each one included a provision to defund the 2010 Affordable Care Act, as Senator Ted Cruz (R-TX) notoriously advocated in a 21-hour Senate speech. Defunding the law was a move that everyone knew was unacceptable to Senate Democrats and the president, and many Senate Republicans expressed dismay at Cruz's move and the House Republicans' response.

During the shutdown, leaders agreed to create a conference committee on the budget resolution to be led by the two budget committee chairs. The two chairs negotiated a two-year deal for spending caps that was adopted in December and set the stage for negotiating an omnibus appropriations measure that would fund the government for the remainder of the fiscal year. Top appropriations leaders negotiated the omnibus measure, encompassing all 12 regular bills, which was added to an already-passed House bill concerning liability for commercial space launches that was before the Senate. The House accepted the enlarged Senate version. The only postpassage action was the exchange of amendments required to approve the new version of the bill. No conference was held.

The 2013–2014 episode illustrates several features of recent appropriations politics. The actions taken by the House to demand the defunding of the health care law were not expected to be successful and were conspicuously designed for political purposes, but they contributed to the government shutdown and crisis negotiations during the fall of 2013. Those negotiations were left to a few top party and committee leaders, who eventually settled on a budget deal and an omnibus appropriations package. The regular bills were not passed, no formal conference committee on the omnibus package was appointed, and influence over the details of the omnibus package flowed through a few leaders. Intense political games were played between the parties, sharp differences over policy delayed action, and control over the final provisions of the spending bill was delegated to a few leaders.

Overall, for the 1961–2014 period, almost 40 percent of all conference committees were associated with appropriations measures. On average, as figure 4.6 shows, the percentage of all conferences that have been appropriations conferences has been higher since the 1980s than it was previously. This is *not* because appropriations conferences are more common. To the contrary, it is largely due to the decline in the number of conferences for other kinds of legislation, a subject that we addressed in chapter 2. With the rise in interparty conflict and Senate obstruction, fewer bills get passed. Those bills that were adopted sometimes were folded into larger measures, which reduced the number of separate bills and contributed to the decline in the number of conferences.

Types of Appropriations Measures and Post-Passage Processes

The relationship between the use of regular bills and conferences is shown in table 4.1 for the entire period considered here. Regular appropriations bills, which originate in the subcommittees of the House and Senate appropriations committees, typically go to conference committee. To deal with a nongermane item or a particularly troublesome issue, a conference report might be accompanied by amendments in disagreement that are then usually handled with an exchange of amendments between the houses.

In the case of non-regular appropriations measures, continuing resolutions are seldom sent to conference. Most short-term continuing resolutions are very brief, merely extending past spending authority at previously established levels and not requiring lengthy negotiations. In contrast, supplemental appropriations bills and the few rescission bills

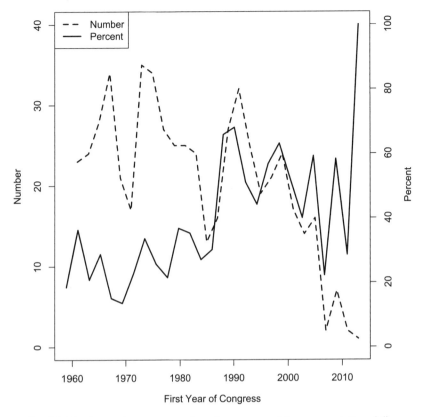

Fig. 4.6. Number and percentage of conferences resolving appropriations bills, 1961–2014. (Compiled by the authors from *CQ Almanac*.)

usually go to conference. The net result is the near even split between conference and simple passage for non-regular appropriations bills that is shown in table 4.1.

An exchange of amendments alone is rare for appropriations measures. For the vast majority of measures, either the measure is a short and simple continuing resolution arranged by top leaders that requires no additional post-passage negotiation or the measure is sufficiently complex that appropriations members want to go to conference to exercise some influence over the legislative details. An exchange of amendments is common after a conference settles a controversial issue or handles a nongermane provision. Such cases are grouped with conferences in table 4.1.

The Structure of Appropriations Conferences

With few exceptions, the structure of appropriations conferences has been a simple one. For regular appropriations bills, conference delegations have been primarily the members of the originating subcommittee with no sub-conference arrangement, and usually the addition of the full committee chair and ranking member. More complex conference delegations have been used only rarely by the House and never by the Senate. The House used limited-purpose conferees 17 times between 1961 and 2014. In six cases, the measure was an omnibus, large continuing resolution, or a large supplemental appropriation that spanned more than one subcommittee or regular appropriations bill. The first two House delegations for appropriations bills illustrate the two main forms that complex conference delegations have taken—the first to deal with a specific controversial issue and the second to manage an omnibus bill.

The first limited-purpose conferees on an appropriations measure were appointed in 1983 for a defense appropriations bill. Edward Boland (D-MA), a member of the full committee but not of the defense subcommittee, and two others were appointed by the House Speaker for the consideration of a provision funding rebels in Nicaragua, an issue that divided liberal Democrats from others. Boland had authored an amendment in 1982 that prohibited funds for the rebels, and the Democratic House and Republican Senate had taken quite different positions on the issue in 1983. Boland and the other Democrat appointed for that issue created a little more support for opposing rebel funding in conference. Boland's presence on the confer-

TABLE 4.1. House-Senate reconciliation method for regular and non-regular appropriations bills, 1961–2012

Method	Regular Appropriations Bills (%)	Non-Regular Appropriations Bills (%)*
Simple—Senate Accepts House Measure	2.3	39.7
Exchange of Amendments	3.5	15.9
Conference or	83.4	42.9
Conference with Exchange of Amendments		
Other	10.8	1.6
Total	100.0	100.0
(N)	(566)	(189)

Note: *Continuing resolutions, rescissions, supplemental appropriations.
Source: Compiled by the authors from CQ Almanac.

ence committee to deal with the issue helped to sell the conference report to House liberals.

The second appropriations measure with a subconference structure was the continuing appropriations resolution passed in 1986. The Democratic House and Republican Senate had failed to pass most regular appropriations bills and a conference was arranged to negotiate with the Senate, as opposed to merely extending past funding levels. The Senate appointed the members of its Committee on Appropriations without any subconference structure. As we report in table 4.2, the House appointed the most senior members of its Committee on Appropriations as conferees for the entire bill (we labeled them "general purpose" in chapter 2) and also created 11 groups, one for each subcommittee and regular appropriations bill, who would join the general conferees in representing the House on matters under each subcommittee's jurisdiction. Technically, the general conferees would vote on each part of a conference report, increasing the number of appropriators who were formally involved in the process of resolving House-Senate differences on each beyond the usual subcommittee members.

In both cases, the House Speaker, Democrat Thomas "Tip" O'Neill, was expanding the range of legislators involved in conference negotiations. In the first case, he made a modest adjustment to the conference delegation to accommodate a colleague who had played a central role on a controversial issue. This was in the spirit of the rule adopted in 1977 that provides that the Speaker should, "to the fullest extent feasible, include the principal proponents of the major provisions of the bill" on conference committees (House Rule I, 11). The large 1986 conference represented an effort to balance the need to get the massive bill passed quickly and the desire to allow subcommittee members to perform their traditional role of representing the House on regular appropriations bills. It was patterned after reconciliation bill conferences, which acquired a complex subconference structure to accommodate the many standing committees that fashioned titles that were then concatenated into a larger bill by the Budget Committee, a process first used in 1980.

Thirteen of the 16 cases of complex House conference delegations for appropriations measures occurred between 1987 and 2007. This was a period of intense party conflict over federal spending and frequently divided party control of the House, Senate, and White House, but the reasons for appointing limited purpose conferees varied as the issues at stake and the policy positions of key players varied. For almost half of the total number of conferences with complex structures, subconferences

TABLE 4.2. House conferees for H.J.Res. 738, continuing appropriations, 1986

For the entire resolution and Senate amendments: Messrs. Whitten, Boland, Natcher, Smith of Iowa, Yates, Obey, Roybal, Bevill, Chappell, Lehman of Florida, Dixon, Fazio, Hefner, Conte, McDade, Myers of Indiana, Miller of Ohio, Coughlin, Young of Florida, Kemp, and Regula.

As additional conferees solely for consideration of Senate amendments within the jurisdiction of the Subcommittee on Agriculture, Rural Development, and Related Agencies, and modifications committed to conference: Messrs. Traxler, McHugh, Akaka, Watkins, and Durbin, Mrs. Smith of Nebraska, Messrs. Rogers, and Skeen.

Solely for consideration of Senate amendments within the jurisdiction of the Subcommittee on the Departments of Commerce, Justice, and State, the Judiciary, and Related Agencies, and modifications committed to conference: Messrs. Alexander, Early, Dwyer, Carr, Mollohan, Rogers, and Michel.

Solely for consideration of Senate amendments within the jurisdiction of the Subcommittee on the Department of Defense, and modifications committed to conference: Messrs. Murtha, Dicks, Wilson, AuCoin, Sabo, Miller of Ohio, and Livingston.

Solely for consideration of Senate amendments within the jurisdiction of the Subcommittee on the District of Columbia, and modifications committed to conference: Messrs. Stokes, Wilson, Sabo, Hoyer, Green, and Wolf.

Solely for consideration of Senate amendments within the jurisdiction of the Subcommittee on Energy and Water Development, and modifications committed to conference: Mrs. Boggs, Messrs. Watkins, and Boner of Tennessee, Mrs. Smith of Nebraska, and Mr. Rudd.

Solely for consideration of Senate amendments within the jurisdiction of the Subcommittee on Foreign Operations, and modifications committed to conference: Messrs. McHugh, Wilson, Gray of Pennsylvania, Mrazek, Edwards of Oklahoma, Lewis of California, and Porter.

Solely for consideration of Senate amendments within the jurisdiction of the Subcommittee on the Department of Housing and Urban Development-Independent Agencies, and modifications committed to conference: Messrs. Traxler and Stokes, Mrs. Boggs, Messrs. Boner of Tennessee, Mollohan, Green, and LeWis of California.

Solely for consideration of Senate amendments within the jurisdiction of the Subcommittee on the Department of the Interior and Related Agencies, and modifications committed to conference: Messrs. Murtha, Dicks, AuCoin, and Loeffler.

Solely for consideration of Senate amendments under the jurisdiction of the Subcommittee on Military Construction, and modifications committed to conference: Messrs. Alexander, Coleman of Texas, Early, Dicks, Edwards of Oklahoma, Loeffler, Rudd, and Lowery of California.

Solely for consideration of Senate amendments under the jurisdiction of the Subcommittee on the Department of Transportation and Related Agencies, and modifications committed to conference: Messrs. Gray of Pennsylvania, Carr, Durbin, Mrazek, Sabo, Pursell, and Wolf.

Solely for consideration of Senate amendments under the jurisdiction of the Subcommittee on Treasury, Postal Service, and General Government, and modifications committed to conference: Messrs. Akaka, Hoyer, Coleman of Texas, Skeen, Lowery of California, and Wolf.

Source: Compiled by the authors from *Calendars of the United States House of Representatives and History of Legislation, Final Edition*, 99th Congress, pp. 18–22.

were created for supplemental appropriations, rescissions, and omnibus bills that addressed subjects under the jurisdiction of many House appropriations subcommittees. For the defense appropriations bill considered in 1988, the usual complement of defense subcommittee members were appointed as House conferees, but they were supplemented with other appropriators on arms control matters because the subcommittee chair did not share the views of a majority of the committee and most House Democrats, who were then the majority party.[1] In 2002, with Republicans in the House majority, the usual defense subcommittee members were appointed to the conference, but the two most senior full committee Republicans and the most senior Democrat were made the exclusive conferees for the purpose of considering supplemental appropriations for a variety of programs. The supplemental funding included funding for the war in Afghanistan and other purposes that were not very controversial but required immediate attention.

The record for post-passage legislating on appropriations measures confirms the proposition that the budget process and partisan conflict reduced the number of measures and reduced the proportion of measures going to conference. Traditional appropriations bills were often delayed or not considered at all in recent decades, forcing the use of continuing resolutions and omnibus measures that sometimes did not go to conference as traditional appropriations nearly always did. Appropriators adhered to traditional patterns in the appointment of subcommittee members to conference and subconference delegations, but ad hoc arrangements became more common as the committee and majority party struggled to find vehicles for omnibus, emergency, and controversial legislation. In many cases, this radically reduced the number of appropriators assigned to conference with responsibility for some issues, and often moved responsibility for negotiating important features of spending policy into the hands of central party and budget leaders.

Budget Measures

From its start in 1974, the congressional budget process was at the center of procedural and partisan battles in Congress. The process was designed to give Congress a mechanism to coordinate annual spending and revenue decisions by, to oversimplify somewhat, (a) adopting a *budget resolution* in the spring that set spending and revenue targets, (b) acting on a variety of spending and revenue bills in the summer, and (c) reconciling all issues through a *reconciliation bill* adopted before the start of the fiscal year on October 1. By focusing on overall spending and revenues, the process was designed to bring about more discipline and provide a means for addressing deficits, an annual shortfall of revenues relative to spending, that were a central political issue in the early 1970s. Few issues are more important in defining the differences between the two parties, and few institutional reforms have changed the rules of the legislative game more than the 1974 act and later changes to it.

Concern about the importance of budget measures under the 1974 process led the House to provide for a rotating membership on its Committee on the Budget. None of its members may serve for more than six out of 10 years. Moreover, to balance its role with other committees and give it more expertise, five of the House Budget Committee's members come from the Committee on Ways and Means, five more from Appropriations, and one from each of the other authorizing committees. The Senate committee does not treat its Budget Committee in these ways—membership is treated much like other important committees. For members of both budget committees, conference committees have long been an important feature of their responsibilities and a source of personal influence.

Budget measures are a high priority for congressional parties and their leaders. Party reputations with the public are greatly influenced by the stances that the parties take on spending, taxes, and budget deficits, as well as their ability to pass legislation in a timely manner. Surely the details of the budget process do not interest most Americans, but the public plainly cares when the complicated budget process is stalled so that spending, tax, or deficit reduction legislation fails to move forward because of the inability of the Congress and president to enact legislation. The result is that party leaders take a keen role in supervising the development and passage of budget measures and are often called upon to negotiate with each other and the president on major budget packages.

The two primary types of budget measures—budget resolutions and reconciliation bills—serve different purposes. The budget resolutions set spending and revenue targets, and also authorize spending and tax bills to be considered. They are reported by the budget committees and do not have the force of law. Reconciliation bills usually focus on deficit reduction. They do so by providing a package of spending cuts, which may include programmatic changes that affect both entitlement and discretionary spending, and often by addressing tax policy. In a few years, reconciliation bills have been used for somewhat different purposes, such as enacting tax cuts. Both kinds of measures are subject to debate and amendment limits in both houses, which protects them from Senate filibusters and improves the odds of passage.

A Brief History

The history of post-passage decision making on budget measures is remarkably straightforward until the turn of the twenty-first century. In table 4.3, the post-passage method is shown for the 1975–2015 period, with conferences split between simple conferences (with no subconferences or limited-purpose conferees) and more complex ones. Budget resolutions involve simple conference structures, with conference delegations composed exclusively of budget committee members in most cases. Reconciliation bills, which package proposals from many committees, are nearly always handled by conference committees with subconference arrangements. Sometimes these conferences have involved a record-setting number of conferees. For the reconciliation bill conference in 1981, the Senate named seven general-purpose conferees from the Budget Committee and 14 subconference groups, most of which had five members, from the various committees with primary responsibility for the 14 titles of the bill. The House named 10 general-purpose conferees and a similar number of subconferences. Conferees for the provisions relevant to the Committee on Education and Labor were divided into nine subconferences. Overall, more than 250 members were appointed to the conference. A similar number of conferees were appointed in 1985 and 1990.

After a run of passing a budget resolution in 23 consecutive years, the House and Senate failed to agree to one in 1998, and then again in 2002, 2006, and 2009–15. Without a budget resolution, no reconciliation bill is authorized. The same conflict over fiscal policy that produced delays, continuing resolutions, and omnibus bills for appropriations also generated stalemate and inaction on budget measures. But budget measures are

TABLE 4.3. House-Senate reconciliation method for budget measures, 1975–2015

Method	Budget Resolutions	Reconciliation Bills
Simple Passage	2	0
Exchange of Amendments	1	0
Conference (Simple)	25	2
Conference (Complex)	1	14
Total	29	16

Source: Compiled by the authors from *CQ Almanac*.

optional for Congress, and the option of not passing a budget resolution and a follow-up reconciliation bill became an acceptable outcome for legislators who were unwilling to compromise. These differences sometimes involved factions within one party or the other, but they always split the two parties.

In 1998, congressional Republicans, in control of both houses, could not agree on accepting the projected budget surplus, making deeper spending cuts, or providing for a tax cut. Moreover, with an election ahead, Senate Republicans did not want a reconciliation bill to make deeper cuts. Without the necessity of passing a budget resolution to authorize a reconciliation bill, the Republican majorities simply let the issue drop. The election was critical to strategic thinking about the budget resolution for some Republicans, but differences within the party in the face of a popular president and budget surplus left the Republican majorities without clear direction.

In the next two decades, interparty and sometimes intraparty factional conflict about fiscal policy produced stalemate and no budget resolution about half of the time. Electoral considerations, as in 1998, were often conspicuously involved, particularly in even-numbered years (2002, 2006, 2010) when the majority party in one or both houses decided to keep budget fights to a minimum and avoid opportunities for the minority to score political points. These were calculations made by, or at least with the heavy participation of, central party leaders. Naturally, the absence of budget resolutions and reconciliation bills trimmed the number of conferences since the late 1990s.

In 2011, House Republicans held the adoption of a bill to increase the federal debt ceiling hostage in their pursuit of sizeable cuts in government spending. The showdown involved negotiations among top party leaders, the president, and other top administration officials. A government shutdown was averted when top party leaders agreed to the terms of the Budget Act of 2011, which increased the debt ceiling and created a special committee charged with devising deficit reduction plans with specific goals by the end of the year. The importance of the effort led the panel to be dubbed the "supercommittee." If the committee failed to produce a plan or Congress failed to adopt it, automatic cuts in discretionary spending (called sequestration) would be imposed for ten years. In fact, Congress failed to pass a plan and sequestration was implemented. The outcome set up years of struggle to negotiate new spending limits in order to avoid the difficult cuts imposed by sequestration.

The immediate effect of the 2011 sequestration process was a continued deadlock over major deficit reduction plans and inaction on budget resolutions. In 2012, the Republican House passed a resolution calling for deeper spending cuts and tax reform, but the Democratic Senate did not take up a budget resolution. In 2013, each house passed a version of a budget resolution, but Republicans insisted on agreement between the top party and budget leaders on the structure of a budget before appointing conferees. No conference committee formed and no appropriations bills were passed. Another government shutdown resulted and was followed by a series of continuing resolutions, as leaders scrambled to avoid the "fiscal cliff"— another round of sequestration cuts and expiring tax laws at the end of the year. Eventually, negotiations between the two budget committees' chairs set appropriations levels for two years, rolling back the sequester levels. Their deal was written as a joint resolution, a measure that goes to the president and has the force of law, rather than a budget resolution, because it was composed of both traditional budget resolution features (spending and revenue targets) and changes in law that would save money to cover the relaxed overall spending targets. With the two-year plan in place, no budget resolution was adopted by both houses in 2014. The Republican House passed a version to show their priorities, but, as expected from the start, the Senate Budget Committee did not produce a budget resolution. With no resolution, there was no 2014 reconciliation bill.

In 2015, House Republican Speaker John Boehner (R-OH) gave up his post in the middle of an intraparty fight about how to use the debt ceiling, appropriations bills, and the expiring two-year spending limits to persuade President Obama to make major concessions on several policies. Boehner had long struggled with members of his party conference, particularly the most conservative Republicans who were organized as the Freedom Caucus in 2015, as he sought to negotiate long-term budget deals with President Obama. The 2015 impasse over spending bills and a reconciliation bill brought matters to a head in August and September as some Republicans spoke about removing Boehner from the speakership. Boehner surprised most observers when, in late September, he announced his plan to resign the speakership.

Boehner's successor, Paul Ryan (R-WI), persuaded his fellow partisans to allow the enactment of a new two-year budget and debt ceiling deal with the president. The deal was negotiated by top party and budget leaders. It was approved without a conference and through an exchange of amendments between the houses. Dozens of federal programs under the jurisdiction of many House and Senate committees were affected, but the committee members seeking to influence the details had to work through the handful of legislators who were constructing the package.

The Budget Measure Patterns

Even with intensified partisan conflict, the House and Senate of the 1980s and 1990s hung on to the formal procedures of the Budget Act of 1974 to pass budget resolutions and reconciliation bills, and House-Senate differences were resolved by conference committees. In the case of budget resolutions, conference committees were limited to budget committee members, although central party leaders supervised the process with care. For reconciliation measures, constructed from the recommendations of many committees, complex subconference structures were used. Subcommittee members were constrained by overall spending reduction requirements, but they were given substantial discretion within those limits.

Since the late 1990s, the pattern has changed. Stalemate between the parties, particularly when there was divided party control or during an election year, frequently yielded failed or feeble attempts to pass budget resolutions. The major budget deals of 2011, 2013, and 2015, which were brought about by interparty and intraparty conflict over the structure of the federal budget, were negotiated by central party and budget leaders.

The budget deals of the last decade contributed to the general patterns in post-passage decision making in several ways. First, the number of separate budget resolutions and reconciliation bills that passed was cut in half. Second, when budget deals were reached, they were translated into legislation by constructing omnibus measures that addressed spending, taxation, and other policies that traditionally had been considered as separate bills. Third, as negotiations became increasingly difficult, a smaller number of members were directly involved in negotiations of a final draft of a budget deal, and, at times, a conference was deemed counterproductive or superfluous.

Tax Measures

The history of tax measures is more complicated than the history of appropriations and budget measures, but is equally important. Tax measures originate in the House Committee on Ways and Means and the Senate Committee on Finance. They come in many sizes—ranging from short bills to change a tax rate to lengthy measures that alter dozens of features of the federal tax code (formally designated Title 26), which is estimated to be about 3.8 million words long.[2] Some federal taxes remain in place until changed, and others have expiration dates that can motivate Congress to enact new legislation. The tax code is almost always controversial for its fairness, complexity, and revenue-generating ability, which makes it one of the most mentioned topics in election campaigns, a popular domain for legislative proposals, and the subject of an uneven flow of legislation through Congress. The parties often place high priority on tax legislation, and, as we observed above, often take very different positions on tax issues.

Here, we focus on "major" tax bills. We do not have a particularly clean definition of what we mean by major, but we will focus on bills that often are called tax "reform" bills or that propose a significant tax hike or reduction. We believe this definition squares with conventional wisdom about what constitutes significant legislation in the domain of tax policy. These bills tend to be quite long and gain action irregularly—only once every year or two, or even less frequently.

The history of major tax measures adds to our understanding of the pattern of post-passage decision making by contributing to our story about the importance of fiscal policy making. Tax bills were always treated as stand-alone measures in the mid-twentieth century. Their importance helped to make the tax-writing committees among the most powerful in Congress. Quite famously, long-time committee chairs Wilbur Mills (D-AR) and Russell Long (D-LA) dominated tax policy in the late 1960s and early 1970s, in major part because of their domination of conference negotiations.

One of the most famous tax bills of the era, the 1963 Kennedy tax cut, illustrates the process typical of post-passage decision making in the 1960s and 1970s. The bill called for a reduction in the high tax rates set during World War II (capital gains tax rates were proposed by the House but rejected by the Senate and opposed by Kennedy), and the measure's success in stimulating the economy has been cited by conservatives as evidence of the value of tax cuts despite the fact that the cuts were not accompanied by corresponding cuts in federal spending. A Democratic Congress followed the traditional legislative process for tax bills, which must originate in the House: House committee approval, House floor approval, Senate committee approval, Senate floor approval, conference, and House and Senate approval of the conference report. The House modified the president's proposal in many ways and the Senate accepted most of the House bill, although a significant number of items were addressed in conference. In the House, many Republicans opposed the bill, instead favoring tying the tax cut to spending cuts to keep the budget balanced. The conference report, which was negotiated primarily by the committee chairs and their staff under the watchful eye of White House representatives, was readily approved by both houses.

Table 4.4 lists the major tax bills in the 1961–2015 period, along with

TABLE 4.4. House-Senate reconciliation method for major tax bills, 1961–2014

Congress	Bill	Bill Title	Reconciliation Method
87	HR10650	Revenue Act of 1962	conference
88	HR8363	Revenue Act of 1963	conference
89	HR8371	Excise Tax Reduction Act of 1965	conference
89	HR12752	Tax Adjustment Act of 1966	conference
91	HR13270	Tax Reform Act of 1969	conference
92	HR10947	Revenue Act of 1971	conference
94	HR2166	Tax Reduction Act of 1975	conference
94	HR10612	Tax Reform Act of 1976	conference
95	HR13511	Revenue Act of 1978	conference
97	HR4242	Economic Recovery Tax Act of 1981	conference
97	HR4961	Tax Equity and Fiscal Responsibility Act of 1982	conference
98	HR4170	Deficit Reduction Act of 1984 (started as Tax Reform Act of 1984)	conference
99	HR3838	Tax Reform Act of 1986	conference
100	HR3545	Omnibus Budget Reconciliation Act of 1987	conference
101	HR5835	Omnibus Budget Reconciliation Act of 1990	conference
102	HR4210	Tax Fairness and Economic Growth Act of 1992	conference
102	HR11	Revenue Act of 1992	conference
105	HR2014	Taxpayer Relief Act of 1997	conference
106	HR2488	Financial Freedom Act of 1999	conference
107	HR1836	Economic Growth and Tax Relief Reconciliation Act of 2001	conference
108	HR2	Jobs and Growth Tax Relief Reconciliation Act of 2003	conference
108	HR4520	American Jobs Creation Act of 2004	conference
108	HR1308	Working Families Tax Relief Act of 2004	conference
109	HR4297	Tax Increase Prevention and Reconciliation Act of 2005	conference
109	HR6111	Tax Relief and Health Care Act of 2006	simple passage
110	HR5140	Economic Stimulus Act of 2008	exchange of amendments
111	HR1	American Recovery and Reinvestment Act of 2009	conference
111	HR4853	Tax Relief, Unemployment Insurance Reauthorization, and Job Creation Act of 2010	exchange of amendments
112	HR3630	Middle Class Tax Relief and Job Creation Act of 2012	conference
113	HR8	American Tax Payer Relief Act of 2012	exchange of amendments

Source: Compiled by the authors from *CQ Almanac*.

the means by which House-Senate differences were resolved. Until very recently, tax bills continued to be negotiated in conference. Conference proceedings on major tax bills usually are accompanied by high-level negotiations with the White House and often involve top congressional party leaders.

The budget process began to affect major tax legislation in a significant way in 1984. In that year, Republican president Ronald Reagan and the Republican Senate decided to enact a deficit reduction package of tax hikes and spending cuts before considering a budget resolution. Known as the "Rose Garden Plan" after its announcement at the White House, the plan was a hybrid package of tax and spending provisions. Negotiations occurred at two levels. The general size and structure of a deficit reduction package was negotiated between the White House and top party and committee leaders during the conference committee phase. Many of the details were negotiated by a large conference committee with 13 House and 8 Senate subconferences of limited-purpose conferees. In fact, the conference looked much like a reconciliation bill conference, with members representing about a dozen House committees and the important addition of appropriations committee members who worked out the details of spending cuts.

Since 1984, tax legislation has been closely tied to the reconciliation process. Because reconciliation bills and their conference reports are considered under debate and amendment limits in both houses, and therefore protected from filibusters in the Senate, tax bill advocates learned to use reconciliation as a means to gain action on their proposals. The 1997 tax bill was the first reconciliation measure devoted entirely to tax cuts, as were the tax cut bills of 2001 and 2003 (the Bush tax cuts). The use of reconciliation procedures for tax cut bills was always combined with conference committee consideration, but it is likely that some smaller tax legislation that would have been considered as separate bills were rolled into the reconciliation measures. In other years, most notably 1987, 1990, and 2005, important tax provisions were incorporated in larger reconciliation bills. In these instances, it is more obvious that tax legislation that previously would have been free-standing bills was incorporated in larger packages, which reduced the number of conferences and limited the number of members negotiating over House-Senate differences.

Since the Great Recession of 2008–9, a period of very sharp partisan conflict, tax legislation has emerged as a part of summit-level negotiations between top congressional leaders and the president under conditions of divided party control of the House, Senate, and White House. In

2008, 2010, and 2012, major budget deals included important tax provisions affecting hundreds of billions of dollars in revenue. These deals were then packaged and passed without conferences and involved pro-forma exchanges of amendments between the houses to get the necessary approvals of the same legislation. The normal process of committee, floor, and conference consideration was collapsed so as to quickly and conveniently finalize action on fragile interparty, interinstitution fiscal policy deals.

In summary, tax committee legislators hung on to conference-dominated post-passage processes until recent years when partisan conflict and divided party control overtook them. Since the 1980s, as partisan differences deepened, the budget process has shaped legislative strategies and several tax bills have been treated as, or incorporated in, reconciliation measures. However, reliance on conferences to work out differences on tax provisions remained the norm only until the Great Recession. In recent years, when partisan gridlock forced innovations in decision-making processes, conferences were discarded in favor of summit negotiations among the top legislative actors that produced packaged deals that were readily enacted. Party-based negotiations replaced committee-oriented conferences.

Defense Authorization Bills

The effects of partisan competition and polarization took longer to take hold in the post-passage politics of major defense policy bills, but they eventually were conspicuously registered there, too. This happened even when the parties differed only on peripheral issues and agreed on the desirability of passing the bills. Interparty competition eventually spurred largely symbolic conflict that led the majority party to give up on conferencing to resolve House-Senate differences and altered who was engaged in the final stages of the legislative process.

Our interest is the modern defense authorization bill. The annual defense authorization bill took form over the decades since the 1950s, when many separate bills on procurement, pay, and other matters were passed. In 1959, Congress, at the behest of the two armed services committees, required an authorization bill to pass before appropriations could be used to procure military weapons and equipment, starting in 1961. The annual "procurement bill" became the most important defense bill in most years. In 1981, the two armed services committees expanded the scope of the annual bill to include the operation and maintenance activities of the armed services, and in doing so created what was renamed the "defense authorization" and is now known as the National Defense Authorization Act.

In every year from 1961 through 2007, the annual procurement or authorization bill was enacted after a conference was held to resolve House-Senate differences. In most cases, negotiations were led by the committee chairs with little direct oversight from party leaders. In a few years (most notably 1978, 1984, 1985, 1988, and 1995), controversies divided the parties and sometimes involved a veto, which led party leaders to play a more prominent role. Divided party control of the White House and Congress was sometimes a factor (1984, 1985, 1995), but not always.

The string of conference-negotiated bills ended in 2008, when inter-party gamesmanship led the majority party to skip a conference. Democrats held House and Senate majorities and Republican George W. Bush was president. Senate Republicans filibustered a motion to go to conference because of their inability to get votes on amendments related to earmarks and offshore oil drilling, but this did not deter Democrats from passing a bill. Knowing that most Republicans actually favored the bill and that the president was going to sign it, the senior Democrats of the two armed services committees resolved the differences between House and Senate versions in private negotiations. The House Democratic leadership then brought the result as a new bill to the floor under suspension of the rules, which bars amendments but requires a two-thirds majority. The revised version easily passed, 392–39, and Senate Republicans allowed the final version to be approved by voice vote. The largely symbolic Senate Republican obstruction to going to conference only had the effect of keeping the Republicans out of a conference on which they did not expect to play a meaningful role anyway.

Two years later, in 2010, a largely partisan divide over the issue of gays in the military—repealing the "don't ask, don't tell" policy—led to delays in Senate consideration of the defense authorization bill. Senators objecting to the repeal blocked cloture on the bill, and eventually repeal proponents agreed to take up that issue in separate legislation. While the bill was hung up in the Senate, the chairs of the two armed services committees reached agreement on all other parts of the bill, introduced their compromise version as a new bill, and had the new bill passed with a quick exchange of amendments without a conference—finally by voice votes in both houses with only two days left in the session. The repeal of "don't ask, don't tell" passed separately. Again, the interplay of the two parties, more than substantive policy problems, caused committee leaders to sidestep the conference process.

In 2013 and 2014, nearly the same process unfolded. In 2013, a Republican filibuster, this time over not getting votes on several amendments, generated a chair-negotiated compromise and easy House and Senate passage of a new bill. In 2014, Senate Majority Leader Harry Reid (D-NV) decided not to bring the defense authorization bill to the floor. The chairs negotiated a compromise version and, with an exchange of amendments, it was passed by wide margins in both houses.

Thus, for defense authorization bills, a long tradition of committee-oriented, conference-based post-passage decision making came to an end in recent years. While defense issues occasionally became quite partisan during the decades since the 1950s, the two armed services committees managed to keep sufficient check on partisanship to maintain the conference as the location for settling House-Senate differences on the annual defense bill. That ended in 2010. The minority party seemed willing to risk losing a role in conference in order to protest its treatment on the Senate floor even when most minority party senators favored the bill. When the protest took the form of preventing cloture, the majority circumvented the process by introducing a new bill that minority party senators, in the closing days of a session, allowed to get a vote and then supported.

Farm Bills

In the mid-twentieth century, federal agriculture policy involved a set of subsidies, price supports, production and import quotas, and other ways of propping up agricultural incomes. Since the end of World War II, during which farm subsidies helped the war effort, agriculture policy has proven controversial and has generated divisions within both parties. Legislators representing rural states and districts tend to back federal efforts to support farm incomes, while other legislators often prefer to reduce the role of the federal government and let the market determine price and supply. In most Congresses, several bills usually were enacted that addressed a variety of commodities and subsidy programs. In 1961 and 1962, the first two years of the Kennedy administration, farm incomes were suffering and omnibus farm bills were enacted that addressed most major farm programs. But problems in the agricultural economy produced continuing demands on Congress to address the issue.

The 1961 and 1962 bills, as for most omnibus farm bills considered through the 1970s, went to conference. Moreover, like most other conference delegations, the conferees were the most senior members of the two originating House and Senate committees—generally, about seven members from each agriculture committee. With few exceptions, these were legislators from agricultural states and districts.

In 1964, Congress enacted the federal food stamp program to assist in food purchases for low-income families. The bill was produced by the agriculture committees, which saw the program as increasing demand for farm products and had the program administered by the Department of Agriculture. Support for the program was largely from Democrats in the House, but there was more bipartisan support in the Senate. The original food stamp bill did not go to conference because the House accepted the Senate's amendments to the House-passed bill, none of which changed the key features of the bill. The Senate had tightened the ban on using food stamps to purchase imported food, and some House members feared that going to conference might weaken the Senate version. The voice votes on the final version in both houses indicated the breadth of support for the bill.

The agriculture committees quickly discovered the value of combining the omnibus farm bills with food stamp authorization, but passing farm bills was seldom easy. In 1965, Congress enacted the Food and Agriculture Act of 1965, which put most farm and food programs on a four-year authorization. Concern about hunger motivated a 1969 bill to increase the food stamp authorization with a bill that did not require a conference—despite the insistence of the House committee chair who wanted to keep the food stamp program in the same bill as the farm programs. Conflict over the direction of farm programs led to a one-year extension in 1969 and eventually a controversial three-year bill passed in 1970, for which a regular conference was held. Regular conferences were held in 1973 and 1977, too, when food and agriculture omnibus bills were passed.

The 1977 House conference delegation involved one set of three limited-purpose conferees, two Democrats and one Republican, for the purpose of dealing with the Food for Peace program. The program provided for the purchase of farm commodities for shipment to needy countries. Since this was a form of foreign aid, the program fell within the jurisdiction of the House Committee on International Relations. The three limited-purpose conferees were the senior International Relations members who were appointed to be the House conferees for the related provisions of the Senate-passed bill. As usual, the Senate had no limited-purpose conferees. In 1981, a conference settled House-Senate differences, and the House again had limited-purpose conferees, one set for the Food for Peace program and two other sets for specific farm issues. Each of the subconferences allowed the non–Agriculture Committee members who authored an important amendment to serve on the conference committee for consideration of those issues (e.g., sugar and peanut programs).

Since the 1980s, farm programs were involved in the budget battles and efforts to cut spending. Several bills, mostly reconciliation bills, altered farm and nutrition programs to reduce spending, which, of course, meant that agriculture programs were handled by a subconference. Nevertheless, the regular farm bills managed to get enacted in 1985, 1989, 1996, 2002, and 2008. The Senate continued to appoint 11 or so Agriculture Committee members as conferees, but House farm bill delegations became more complex as the bills began to affect the jurisdictions of a wider range of committees. The 2008 House delegation included 12 sets of conferees appointed for limited purposes.

In 2013, the path for the regular omnibus bill was complicated by the fiscal policy fight that produced a 16-day government shutdown in October. The 2008 authorization expired in 2012, and, because of significant differences between the Republican House and Democratic Senate, a new long-term authorization could not be passed. Instead, a one-year extension was adopted in January 2013 (months after the 2008 authorization had expired) as a part of the larger "fiscal cliff" deal negotiated by top leaders. Later in 2013, the House turned down its committee's omnibus farm bill, primarily over the issue of spending on the Supplemental Nutrition Assistance Program (the new name for the food stamp program), which led the House to pass separate farm and food bills, while the Senate passed a comprehensive version. The two House bills and one Senate bill went to conference, which settled the differences and led to the enactment of a five-year extension of the farm and food programs.

The history of farm bills shows a dogged effort on the part of agriculture committee leadership to use conferences to finalize the details of the bills. Budget politics and partisan differences intervened in recent decades, which caused several delays in getting the regular omnibus farm bill passed. Nevertheless, agriculture committee members pressed to get the bills considered and used the traditional conference, modified to accommodate multiple committee interests in the House, whenever possible even under conditions of bitter partisan warfare going on around them on broader fiscal policy issues.

Conclusion

Congress's post-passage decision-making processes, we have argued, are shaped by party and committee leaders who accept traditional processes but adapt them to meet the challenges associated with achieving their policy and electoral goals. In recent decades, as interparty competition has become more intense, divided party control has become more common and future majority control has been in doubt, making electoral goals and the symbolic actions pursued to achieve them a higher priority. At the same time, deeply polarized parties have made compromise across parties and institutions more difficult, delaying decisions and creating a series of crises over deadlines. These conditions have generated less minority party cooperation and more minority party obstruction, more purely symbolic floor activity, and fewer rewards for the hard work of building cross-party, cross-institution support for legislation. Moreover, key policy decisions have been pushed into the laps of central party leaders more frequently and time constraints have minimized the time of negotiations. In this context, party and committee leaders have scrambled to find the procedural means to achieve a difficult mix of policy and electoral objectives, and have often given up on traditional conferences as the means for finalizing the details of legislation.

In this chapter, we have observed that policy domains vary in their centrality to the partisan warfare of the last two decades. Fiscal policy measures—budget resolutions, reconciliation bills, appropriations bills, and tax bills—were at the center of partisan battles and subject to the budget process rules adopted in 1974 and modified several times since then. Traditional ways of legislating were set aside repeatedly to accommodate summit agreements, which, at times, were translated into legislation and enacted without further committee consideration or conferences. Spending and tax bills that traditionally were considered as separate measures were wrapped into omnibus measures, which reduced the number of bills going to conference, reduced the number of committee members involved in negotiations, and increased the importance of adhering to the terms set out in summit agreements. In several recent years, the money committees, and the conferences associated with them, lost much of their significance.

Until recently, legislating on the major defense and agriculture authorization legislation generally took the traditional path through committees, floors, and conference. Support for defense authorization bills was usually bipartisan and agriculture legislation often internally divided both parties. In both cases, the parent committees had a tradition of limiting partisanship and protecting the committee role in shaping policy. Then, both agriculture and defense domains have been drawn into the fiscal policy battles by virtue of the spending implications of those programs, and they have been subjected to partisan maneuvering. As a result, conferencing has collapsed at times in these domains, too.

FIVE

Concluding Thoughts

It is challenging, and perhaps a bit awkward, to write about an isolated stage in the legislative process. Developments in American and congressional politics more generally are bound to influence the strategies that legislators and other interested players pursue when they are plotting the process for enacting or blocking legislation. The post-passage processes, our focus in this book, are shaped by what happens in the House and Senate prior to passing legislation. It is inevitable, then, that the forces that shape House and Senate politics more generally are registered in the record of post-passage politics, too.

It also is awkward to write about such an important subject without saying more than we have about the emotional or psychological side of congressional politics. The intense emotions generated by protracted, acute competition for control of Congress, the deepening policy differences between the parties, the exclusion of the minority from meaningful participation in crafting legislation, and knee-jerk minority obstructionism are real. There is little doubt that the emotional response to the partisan warfare of the last few decades has been very strong at times and perhaps contributed to the strong partisan orientation of legislating in recent decades that has reshaped the post-passage process.

We also are guilty of describing the developments in post-passage politics dispassionately, but we nonetheless acknowledge the importance of these dynamics. We conclude by summarizing our findings and making some observations that are more normative in nature.

What We Found

We have emphasized several patterns in the methods used to resolve House-Senate differences in the past six decades. First, intra- and inter-interparty competition have driven changes in post-passage processes. Factionalism among House majority party Democrats in the early 1970s generated pressures to break up monopolies over legislative jurisdiction enjoyed by senior committees members, create multiple committee bills, expand the number of conferees, and resolve House-Senate differences in multi-committee conferences. In recent decades, party interests—driven by long-term party competition for control of Congress and more deeply polarized parties—have overwhelmed the traditional committee-oriented, conference-based post-passage processes and led to the near disappearance of conference committees.

Second, we have discovered a general pattern in majority party bias in conferences. It is a bias grounded in the committee and party foundations of conference membership. We also have observed the patterns predicted by the changing political environment of congressional policy making. More intense partisan competition and deeper party polarization are associated with greater pro-majority-party bias in conferences. While conferences themselves fell victim to those forces, with majority parties turning to other post-passage strategies across successive waves of change, the conferences that remained exhibited more bias.

Third, we confirmed that post-passage processes in policy domains that are the most central to partisan warfare have experienced more radical change than other important policy domains. The traditional use of conference committees was set aside repeatedly for final action on fiscal policy measures (budget measures, appropriations bills, and tax bills), which reflected the assertion of party interests, the involvement of top party leaders, and the loss of influence for the budget, appropriations, and tax-writing committees. In contrast, defense and agriculture authorization legislation generally took the traditional path through conference. In recent Congresses, both defense and agriculture measures have been overtaken by fiscal policy battles and partisan maneuvering and suffered a decline in conferencing, too.

A Caution about the "Regular Order"

While we do not find most of the congressional rhetoric about "regular order" persuasive, we do believe that procedural changes of the kind we report have consequences for the policy location and quality of legislative outcomes. By "regular order," members of Congress and other observers usually mean the standard legislative process during the middle decades of the twentieth century. That process was a decentralized one centered in the many committees of the House and Senate, and it produced few omnibus measures. Committee chairs, who acquired their posts through seniority, firmly controlled the activities of most committees. Legislative details were written in committee markups and seldom successfully challenged on the floor of either house, expert staffs were housed in committees, and House-Senate differences on important legislation were resolved in conference committees run by those same committee chairs. The advantages of this process were that it encouraged legislators to develop expertise relevant to their committee work, allowed policy specialists to dominate the process, kept partisan politics to relatively few issues, and encouraged meaningful deliberation among committee experts at all stages in the process.

The demise of committee-oriented decision making and the "regular order" is decried by many. Conservative House Republicans who urged their Speaker, John Boehner, to resign in 2015 insisted on a return to regular order, which they believed would give them more voice in House decision making. Senate Majority Leader Mitch McConnell, upon his party's rise to majority status after the 2014 elections, promised a return to regular order in the Senate, which meant relying more on committees, passing all regular appropriations bills, minimizing the number of bills filibustered on the Senate floor, and sending important bills to conference.

Of course, neither the Constitution nor congressional rules establish a "regular order." Congressional rules facilitate committee-oriented decision making, but those rules are created by each house to suit the needs of members, can be set aside by each house, and include alternative methods for legislating. There is nothing improper about using ping-pong methods or writing new bills rather than creating conference committees to resolve differences between the houses. Nevertheless, every procedure has its value and the move away from conferences has risks for Congress (Oleszek 2008). The problem is not that the move away from conferences violates a rule or the Constitution; it does neither. The important issue is whether the institution and the public are well served or harmed by the changes in common practice.

Undermining Committee Expertise and Power

The move from a committee-oriented to a party-oriented policy-making process in Congress threatens to shift primary responsibility from legislators with policy expertise to legislators with political expertise. We recognize that high-quality legislative output is a function of both policy and political expertise, but the relative emphasis on these two qualities shifts as party leaders become relatively more important than committee members in writing the details of legislation. This is intended, of course. It is the product of giving electoral challenges more emphasis after years of competition for control of Congress and seeing little value in committee deliberations involving members of both parties after years of deepening party polarization over substantive issues.

In time, the focus on party-based policy making and a lack of reliance on committees to write legislation may reduce the incentive for legislators to develop genuine policy expertise. In fact, party leaders still turn to committee leaders and their staffs to devise legislative language, but rank-and-file committee members are often bystanders to the process. Devoting time to mastering a subject and consulting with staff and outside experts on the subject becomes far less valuable to a committee member who discovers that the relevant choices will be made by non-committee members the bulk of the time.

The challenges to committee-based expertise are most important for the committees with jurisdiction over issues of most interest to the parties that were likely to go to conference in the past. As we saw in chapter 4, the committees most affected are the money committees, which have long been considered the most powerful committees. The shift to party-based decision making has, therefore, been particularly pronounced on the contours of fiscal policy, since it has affected the power of these committees most dramatically.

Undercutting the Transparency of the Process

Many of the rules governing conferences were intended to enhance the transparency of post-passage proceedings for the broader membership and the public. Both houses have rules that require meetings of conference committees to be open to the public and provide special procedures for closing conference sessions. Furthermore, conferences are required to provide joint explanatory statements that detail the major features of the conferees' agreements. The House rule (Rule XXII, 7(e)), much like the Senate rule, requires that the "statement shall be sufficiently detailed and explicit to inform the House of the effects of the report on the matters referred to conference." House and Senate layover rules give legislators time to read the reports and explanatory statements before voting on them on the floor. And, of course, the identities of the conferees and the signatories to conference reports—the conferees who approve the reports—are public information as well.

Taking policy choices out of the hands of committees and conferences and moving them to new legislation or amendments between the chambers changes the documentation of policy choices and undermines many of the intended goals of transparency set out by chamber rules. Measures devised by party leaders are unlikely to have lengthy legislative histories in print. Moreover, the identity of the key players involved in devising these measures is not officially recorded, and most of the negotiating action takes place out of the public view. Legislators, affected interests, executive agency officials, and the courts have less guidance about the rationale and implications of legislative provisions when the committee- and conference-based processes are not used.

Excluding the Minority Party

Many of the rules governing conferences were designed to give legislators an opportunity to instruct conferees and challenge conferees' decisions, and therefore give the minority party some voice in the post-passage process. In the House, a minority party member is guaranteed an opportunity to offer a "motion to instruct" conferees. The motion is not binding on conferees, but it gives the minority party an opportunity to put all members on the record regarding the issue subject to the instructions. The House also has a motion to recommit a conference report with instructions. And a variety of points of order may be made for violating rules governing the content of conference reports. In the last two decades, the minority party has more frequently exploited these opportunities to force the majority party to muster a majority in opposition to these motions and to cast votes that might be politically embarrassing for some legislators.

Of course, nothing in congressional rules guarantees minority party members a meaningful role in post-passage negotiations. Even the use of conference committees is no guarantee. When the same party controls

both houses, minority party complaints about being excluded from informal discussions held by majority party conferees have been common for
several decades. Nevertheless, conference committees, at least formally,
create the opportunity for meaningful minority party participation. The
move to party-based negotiations often gives the minority party in both
houses little direct role in post-passage deliberations, as it undercuts the
minority protections built into House rules. For instance, there are no
motions to instruct associated with amendments between the chambers
or when a new bill is brought to the floor, such as a reconciliation bill, to
embody House-Senate compromises.

Chamber rules matter. In the Senate, in contrast to the House, a motion
to go to conference and a motion to consider a conference report can be
filibustered, giving a large and cohesive minority party considerable influence.[1] Taking up House-Senate compromises as amendments between the
houses or as a fresh bill can further limit the number of opportunities for
minority obstruction.

Squeezing Deliberation

The two houses of Congress evolved substantially different methods of
decision making. The larger House limits debate on most matters and
empowers the Rules Committee to propose bill-by-bill limits. Further, the
House bars nongermane amendments in committee and on the floor. Full
discussion of most issues is left to committee rooms, and even there the size
of committees limits how much time individual legislators can speak in a
public forum. The Senate allows unlimited debate and amendments on the
floor for most bills, with budget measures being the most important exception. This enables filibusters, but it also facilitates more open discussion of
issues. On the face of it, more deliberation occurs on the Senate floor than
the House floor, but House members, with fewer committee assignments
than senators, may have more time to devote to committee discussions.

Conference committees bring legislators from these two settings
together. In most cases, the conferees are committee members with considerable policy expertise who represent a wide range of interests. They are
usually supported by sizable, specialized staffs with ready access to executive branch and outside experts. Policy, political, and technical weaknesses
in legislation have a chance to be discovered and repaired in discussions
among conferees and staff.

A good case can be made that a post-passage process that is run by party leaders lacks the range of safeguards built into the more traditional committee-oriented process. The conference process can fail to meet standards for adequate deliberation, too, but, compared with a process that takes place largely in party leaders' offices, the conference process gives more members a formal role in the process.

Biasing Policy Outcomes

While we do not directly measure the spatial locations of policy outcomes in this project, a difficult task to be sure, we can nonetheless learn something about the policy implications of changing practices in post-passage politics from the preceding analyses. Since we cannot measure policy outcomes directly, the ensuing conversation is admittedly more speculative than others. Nonetheless, we believe that the policy implications of post-passage decision making are an important topic worthy of more detailed future study.

We believe our study offers two particularly important insights for understanding the policy implications of the documented changes in post-passage politics. For one, we observe a precipitous decline in the use of conference over recent decades that appears to be the culmination of changes in the institutional and partisan milieu. Second, as shown in chapter 3, conference delegation medians tend not to be as extreme in the policy space as the party medians, which we can safely assume are the positions pursued by party leaders when they choose more party-motivated methods of post-passage resolution in lieu of conference committees.

It seems reasonable to conclude from these points that recent decisions to use alternative methods of intercameral conciliation likely lead to more extreme (and biased) policy outcomes. This conclusion is also consistent with the broader notion that partisan competition and polarization motivate parties to more aggressively pursue their policies. We argue that these changes in post-passage decision making are simply one such avenue through which the parties are able to do so. Therefore, the changes observed have potentially important normative implications for policy outcomes—most notably, that decreased reliance on conference committees has likely resulted in policies that, on average, are less representative of the American electorate.

Our Theme

Congressional policy-making processes are always evolving. Legislators adjust both the formal and informal processes to meet their needs. The institutions that they inherit limit their options to some degree and condition how they adjust to new political circumstances. The major changes in political circumstances of recent decades—intensifying party competition for the control of Congress, deepening partisan polarization, long periods of divided party control of the House, Senate, and presidency—reshaped nearly every aspect of the legislative process and eventually produced a dramatic drop in the frequency of using conference committees to resolve House-Senate differences.

There is continuing interest by members of both houses to return to a more committee-oriented process that includes conferences. Rank-and-file legislators have important interests at stake in the outcomes of partisan warfare, but their individual role in the process is reduced. For now, it appears that their interest in returning to the conference process will have to wait until the larger environment of partisan conflict changes. The return of conference committees would be facilitated by softening partisanship and abating partisan polarization that would allow committee leaders to operate more independently of central party leaders. A return to regular use of conferences for major legislation would get a significant boost with a return to frequent one-party control of the House, Senate, and presidency, which would probably be accompanied by reasonably safe majorities in Congress.

Appendix

Part A. How Conference Works

The rules and procedures surrounding the conference committee are extensive. To quote Tiefer (1989, 768), "In some respects, conference procedure involves the most formal, complex, and technical of all procedural rules." As such, this appendix offers merely a glimpse into the formal procedures surrounding the conference and discusses some of the informal practices that have emerged over time. A full account of all the technical details and practices relating to conference would require volumes and would be beyond the scope of this appendix. Of particular importance, however, are those procedures that inform the theoretical discussions presented in the main chapters. We consider conference procedures and practices in three basic stages—pre-conference, conference, and post-conference.

Pre-Conference Stage

In order for a conference to be needed, differences between House and Senate passed versions of legislation must first arise. Following the emergence of legislative conflict, the chambers must each carry out three steps in order for a conference to convene: formal disagreement, agreement to go to conference, and appointment of conferees. In the first step, the chambers establish their formal disagreement with the other chamber's proposal. Next, the chambers must agree to hold a conference to resolve the formal disagreement that was previously acknowledged. And, finally, each chamber must appoint a delegation of its members to go to conference.

Both chambers must first agree to disagree. A chamber can establish its formal disagreement to the other chamber's proposal by either a motion to "insist" on the amendment(s) it has made to the other chamber's bill or a motion to "disagree" with the other chamber's amendment(s) to its bill.[1] In establishing the disagreement, the chambers need not use exclusively disagreeing motions. Rather, chambers may agree with portions of the other chamber's amendments, but disagree with others. Provided that there is a mutual disagreement on at least one amendment, the "stage of disagreement" is entered. It should be noted that only those amendments in disagreement are technically committed to conference.

Entering into the "stage of disagreement" is considerably different between the chambers. House procedure entails a more complicated route to executing this critical first step. The principal hurdle in establishing disagreement in the House is that Senate amendments to the House's bill lack privilege. The bill, with the Senate changes, is placed on the Speaker's table upon arriving back in the House, and bringing it to the floor for consideration involves further action. There are only four ways in which a bill with Senate amendments can be brought to the floor: unanimous consent, suspension of the rules, a special rule from the Rules Committee, or via House Rule XXII.

By far the most common method of doing this is unanimous consent (Longley and Oleszek 1989; Tiefer 1989). However, there are cases in which members object, requiring other means of bringing the legislation to the floor. With two-thirds support of the membership, the bill can be taken from the Speaker's table and brought to the floor under suspension of the rules. However, if the measure in question is a divisive one, then a super-majority may also be difficult to attain. Special rules, on the other hand, require a lower threshold for support. The Rules Committee has the ability to formulate a rule by simple resolution that allows non-privileged measures to be brought to the floor. This includes Senate amendments. This method relies heavily upon the Rules Committee to cooperate in issuing such a rule. At periods in history, however, the Rules Committee proved to be quite unaccommodating. Such was the case in 1960, when the Rules Committee refused to report a rule to send the Federal-Aid-To-Education Act, which had passed the Senate, to the floor for consideration. Concerned over the Rules Committee's ability to block legislation from going to the floor,[2] the House created Rule XXII (then Rule XX) in 1965 (Tiefer 1989). House Rule XXII[3] permits a member of the committee of jurisdiction, with the approval of her or his panel, to offer a privileged motion that simultaneously establishes a "stage of disagreement" and either requests or agrees to conference.

Entering the "stage of disagreement" has important implications for the House. Once a formal disagreement has been established, the Senate's amendments are privileged (Longley and Oleszek 1989). Therefore, members may proceed to other motions with relative ease. In addition, after entering the "stage of disagreement" the precedence of motions is changed. Preceding disagreement, precedents give priority to motions that perfect the bill, whereas motions that encourage agreement between the chambers are given precedence after disagreement has been established (Longley and Oleszek 1989; Bach 2001). For instance, prior to the stage of disagreement the motion to concur with amendments (first in order of precedence) takes precedence over the motion to concur (second). After disagreement, however, the motion to recede and concur (first) is given priority over the motion to recede and concur with amendments (second) (Rybicki 2015, 11).[4]

In the Senate, House amendments to a Senate bill are privileged, and therefore the Senate does not encounter the same complications as the House in bringing legislation to the floor. Rather, a motion to dispose of the amendments of the House can be brought forward by any senator, and approved of by majority vote.[5] While the Senate rules privilege the consideration of bills that have passed both chambers, making the motion to consider nondebatable, the motion preceding the conference is subject to debate. Prior to filibuster reforms in 2013, there were three such motions—a motion to disagree with the House amendments, a motion to request conference, and a motion to appoint conferees—which gave senators opposed to the measure multiple opportunities to obstruct. These reforms streamlined the process by combining the motions into a single step, thereby reducing the opportunity for obstruction.[6] While it is rare for obstruction to occur on this motion, it is possible for senators hoping to derail a measure to prevent a conference committee from convening by filibustering the motion. Such was the strategy of Republican senators who opposed campaign finance reform legislation (S. 3) in the 103rd Congress. In the hope of defeating a largely Democratic initiative, GOP senators waged a filibuster on the motions preceding conference (Oleszek 2008; Smith 2014). They were successful in killing the bill.

Even prior to the 2013 filibuster reforms, the motion to request or agree to conference was, in practice, considered jointly with the motion to disagree. Most often, the motions were offered in the same breath. Typically, the motion offered was in this form: "Mr. President, I move that the Senate insist on its amendments (disagree with the amendments of the House) and request (agree to) a conference with the House." The only difference in the House is that a motion to consider this legislation (via unanimous consent or other method) must precede the joint motion. The combination of these motions has become so common that, in the House, the joint motion is recognized as taking precedence over a simple motion to disagree.

> It was formerly held that a motion to send to conference yielded to the simple motion to disagree, or to insist (see Cannon's Procedure in the House of Representatives, p. 120). In current practice, however, the compound motion to disagree to Senate amendments and request or agree to a conference, or to insist on House amendments and request or agree to a conference, has replaced the two-step procedure for getting to conference and, because it brings the two Houses together, takes precedence over simple motions to insist or disagree (or to adhere).[7]

The order with which the chambers request conference is of consequence, and may influence a chamber's decision to combine or keep separate the motions to disagree and request conference. In practice, the chamber that asks for conference is last to act on the consideration of the conference report (Longley and Oleszek 1989). Therefore, a chamber may pass a motion to disagree with the other chamber's amendments but not ask for a conference in the hopes that the other chamber will initiate the request and go last in the consideration of the conference report. Alternatively, desire to act last on the conference report may prompt a chamber to package the motions. The chambers may be interested in the order that the conference report is considered for reasons as mundane as time constraints. On the other hand, the order with which the conference report is taken up in the chambers may have important implications for its likelihood of success. The chamber that is first to act on the conference report can act on it in three ways: accept the report, reject it, or recommit it to the conference. If the first-acting chamber accepts the report, the conference committee is dissolved and the second chamber can only accept or reject the conference report (ibid.). Strategic considerations may lead a chamber to act first on the conference report if it is uncertain that the other chamber will pass the report. With fewer procedural options available to it, greater attention from outside sources (e.g., lobbyists or the media), and the momentum of the first-acting chamber's passage of the report, the second-acting chamber may be pressured to act favorably on the conference report (ibid.).

Prior to appointing conferees, both chambers have the option to offer a motion to instruct their own conferees.[8] The motion is an effort made by a chamber to instruct its delegation's conferees to take certain positions when bargaining in conference. The instruction, however, is limited to only those actions that are in order without the instruction (Tiefer 1989). Therefore, instructions cannot ask conferees to insert provisions not committed to them in conference or remove provisions already agreed to by both chambers. A chamber may, for example, instruct its conferees to insist on a particular amendment it had passed.

The motion to instruct conferees is not commonly used in either chamber, but it is used more often in the House than the Senate (Tiefer 1989).[9] In part, their lack of use is a function of the motion's limited purpose. Specifically, instructions to conferees are not binding. As such, no point of order can be raised against a conference report that deviates from the instructions, and conferees who do not carry out the wishes of their chamber are not subject to any sanction (ibid.). Thus, the motion to instruct has been appropriately described as "pious hope" (Longley and Oleszek 1989, 186).

The final, and perhaps most important, pre-conference step is the appointment of the conferees. The House and Senate have different formal rules that govern this process. In the House, the Speaker is granted broad authority to appoint conferees. This is a power that survived the rules changes of 1911, which curtailed the Speaker's authority to make committee appointments (Tiefer 1989). House Rule I,[10] which gives the Speaker the sole authority to appoint conferees, places few restrictions on her or him in carrying out this task. Technically, the Speaker need only consider her or his own preferences when deciding whom to send to conference, since the rule does not require any chamber approval. So broad is the Speaker's authority over the appointment process that she or he may even manipulate the delegation after the initial appointment by removing or adding conferees.[11]

The rule does place one formal constraint on the Speaker's selection of conferees. The Speaker is to "appoint no less than a majority who generally supported the House position." Furthermore, the rule states that the Speaker "shall name those who are primarily responsible for the legislation" and "principal proponents of the major provisions of the bill or resolution passed or adopted by the House." In practice, however, the Speaker is given a tremendous amount of flexibility in her or his adherence to this component of the rule. In large part, the Speaker has considerable latitude because the rule grants her or him the authority to determine what constitutes "general support" and to define the "House position" (Longley and Oleszek 1989). And rarely are these matters self-evident. The looseness with which the Speaker adheres to these requirements also stems from the fact that there are no formal mechanisms through which the chamber is able to overturn the Speaker's appointments (ibid.). Rather, the Speaker makes the final decision as to whether or not she or he has properly carried out the appointment process under House rules. Despite instances in which members have expressed disapproval of the Speaker's appointments, there has never been a reversal of the Speaker's appointment decisions (ibid.).

In the Senate, the formal rules that govern the appointment of Senate conferees are identical to the guidelines for standing committee appointments. Specifically, Senate Rule XXIV[12] provides for the election of conferees by the whole body. If the Senate so chooses, it may elect each individual conferee by majority vote. Thus, unlike the House, the Senate body technically possesses the authority in the conferee appointment process. In practice, however, the Senate almost always relinquishes this power to the presiding officer by unanimous consent, and, in so doing, the chamber authorizes the presiding officer to appoint conferees (Rybicki 2015). The presiding officer, as will be discussed in more detail below, does not exercise any independent influence on the process, and therefore delegating this power to the presiding officer is of minimal cost to the chamber. A benefit of this action is a more expeditious appointment of conferees than would occur if the chamber chose to elect each conferee on an individual basis.

Despite the formal rules that surround the appointment of conferees in both chambers, the reality of the conference appointment process is that the presiding officers in both chambers closely adhere to norms of appointment that minimize their role in deciding who will serve on the conference. In practice, the chair of the committee of jurisdiction usually prepares a list, or slate, of recommended conferees, which is then presented to the presiding officer. In the Senate, the presiding officer always accepts this slate, and therefore exercises little discretion in the process (Bach 2001). While the Speaker rarely deviates from the recommendations of the committee chair, slates carry less weight in the House than they do in the Senate. When the Speaker becomes involved in the appointment process it is typically limited, amounting to one or two additions (Longley and Oleszek 1989). In general, though, the Speaker accepts the slate proposed by the committee chair as is.

While committee chairs have considerable discretion in determining the composition of the slate, they are not completely unconstrained.

Rather, a combination of rules and norms serve as guidelines for appointing conferees. Perhaps the most important norm that governs conference appointments is that conferees come from the committee of jurisdiction. Therefore, it is rare for a committee chair to appoint a member not belonging to the committee over which she or he presides. Access to conference is very much viewed as a right of committee membership.

In deciding which committee members will go to conference, it is common practice for the chair to consult with the ranking minority member in the naming of the minority conferees. And it is typical for the chair to outright accept the recommendations of the ranking member (Longley and Oleszek 1989). Therefore, in practice, the chair only selects the majority party members from the committee that will go to conference. This is, however, an important task given that conference bargaining operates by majority rule within delegations (see conference stage).

Committee chairs have long observed committee seniority as a guide for appointing committee members to conference. At periods in congressional history, conference appointments were virtually automated according to seniority on the parent committee. In recent decades, however, this norm has been softened somewhat. The growth of the subcommittee system in the 1970s (Davidson 1981) led to an increase in appointments by subcommittee seniority (Tiefer 1989). Since committee seniority is dispersed across subcommittees, given that senior committee members go to different subcommittees to serve as chair, appointments made according to subcommittee seniority give junior members of the committee more access to conference. The existence of two norms that do not necessarily produce the same results gives committee chairs some additional flexibility in the appointment process (ibid.).[13]

In addition, it is the practice for committee chairs to recommend the appointment of committee members who have been particularly prominent in the formation of the legislation, irrespective of seniority. At least in the House, an individual who has been central to legislation can stake formal claim to conference appointment. In addition, failing to appoint a prominent committee member may be viewed as a slight against that member (Longley and Oleszek 1989). A member who believes she or he has wrongly been omitted from participating in conference may choose to orchestrate opposition to the conference report or may challenge future measures of importance to the committee or committee chair.

The committee chair is usually charged with determining the delegation's size. The size of the conference delegation is quite flexible, as there are no formal rules or norms that guide this decision. Recent trends have been toward increasing numbers. In 1971, the average size of a conference delegation (House and Senate) was eight. In recent years, the size of a House delegation has more than tripled to twenty-five. Senate delegations have also increased, although less drastically. Today, the average Senate delegation has roughly twelve conferees (Oleszek et al. 2016).

A few important factors influence the committee chair's decision regarding the size of the conference delegation. To begin, committee chairs can use the size of the delegation to influence its ideological balance (Van Beek 1995). Suppose, for example, that the three most senior members on a committee are likely to oppose a measure in conference that the committee chair supports. However, the remaining ten members of lesser seniority have expressed support for that measure. If the committee chair wishes to adhere to the norm of seniority but also strongly desires the passage of the measure, she or he may choose to appoint at least seven conferees so that a majority of the delegation supports the measure. If, on the other hand, the committee chair opposes the bill, she or he may select a delegation of no larger than five. Thus, the chair's policy position, in conjunction with adherence to the norm of seniority, may influence the size of the conference delegation.

In determining the delegation size, a chair must also consider the effect it will have on the bargaining process. A particular advantage of conference is the reduced number of preferences that must be satisfied. Increasing the number of conferees, then, has the potential of making the conference less efficient. Furthermore, large numbers complicate the planning of logistical details (such as scheduling) surrounding the negotiations (Longley and Oleszek 1989).

Another important factor in establishing the composition of the conference delegation is the ratio of majority to minority party members. Tradition dictates that the chair appoint members according to the party ratio in the chamber (Tiefer 1989). In practice, however, this is not strictly adhered to. Studies of party representation on conference delegations find that the majority party consistently possesses a disproportionate advantage of conference seats (Vogler 1970; Vander Wielen and Smith 2011).

Committee chairs do not, however, make these decisions in a vacuum. Party leaders may also play an active role in influencing a chair's decision. This is particularly true when the legislation going to conference is widely considered to be important. In addition, party leaders become involved in the appointment process when the legislation affects the jurisdiction of more than one committee (Bach 2001). When legislation of this nature arises, party leaders coordinate the appointments from the various committees, and, in so doing, may consider the ideological balance of the resulting delegation (Sinclair 2012b). Multiple-committee delegations are now relatively common,[14] and in some cases can include several different committees. In 1981, for instance, the conference committee on the Fiscal 1982 Omnibus Reconciliation Bill (H.R. 2982) had conferees from seventeen House committees and fourteen Senate committees (Tiefer 1989).

Multiple-committee conferences have given rise to the appointment of conferees with limited as opposed to general authority. Conferees with limited authority (called limited-purpose conferees) are not permitted to negotiate on all provisions of the legislation, and, in the House, can vote on only those matters within their authority.[15] When legislation touching the jurisdiction of multiple committees goes to conference, it is common for each committee to appoint conferees with the authority to negotiate on only those matters that fall within the committee's jurisdiction (Bach 2001). The conference delegations need not be composed of members from multiple committees for conferees to have limited authority. Furthermore, it is possible to have a mix of limited and general purpose conferees on a given conference committee. In fact, the flexibility involved in designating an appointee's authority in conference gives committee chairs and party leaders the ability to manipulate the balance of the committee. Suppose, for example, that a committee member was out of step with the committee chair and party on a single, yet noteworthy, provision to be considered in conference. If, for some reason, the chair believed that this member could present a threat to the legislation in conference, given her or his opposition to the provision, it is within the chair's power to preclude the conferee from negotiating on said provision. Such was the case in 1989 when Congress was considering legislation to overhaul the savings and loan industry (H.R. 1278). The legislation touched the jurisdiction of five House committees— Banking, Judiciary, Ways and Means, Government Operations, and Rules. Banking Committee chairman Henry Gonzalez (D-Texas) was allowed to appoint all the members of his committee (55 total). However, Gonzalez was concerned over positions that some of his members had adopted, and decided to assign each of the members to negotiate on one of five sections of the legislation. When asked why he did this, Gonzalez "conceded that he organized the smaller groups to tilt the balance on certain issues and help guarantee that his views would prevail" (Cranford 1989).

Conference Stage

Once conference has been agreed to and the conferees selected, the next step is the conference, or bargaining, stage. There are remarkably few formal rules that govern the process of reconciling the differences between the chambers. In fact, much of the activity surrounding this stage is improvised. In large part, the details of the bargaining process remain flexible so as to allow conferees to select arrangements on a case-by-case basis that best facilitate conciliation.

The initial step in the conference stage is the selection of a conference chair. Each delegation enters this stage with a designated leader. The presiding officer is formally responsible for selecting which appointee will lead the delegation.[16] However, in practice the chair of the standing committee is likely to select herself/himself or a subcommittee chair for this role (Tiefer 1989). Although the conference chair is chosen from the two delegations' leaders, there is no formal process that guides this decision. Rather, each conference may choose its own method for determining who will be chair. Some committees that repeatedly meet in conference over recurring measures make arrangements to alternate leadership, but such arrangements are not feasible for all committees. At times, the selection of the conference chair has been heated, and party leaders have been needed to settle the disputes (Oleszek et al. 2016).[17]

Emotions can run high on the selection of the conference chair because the member in this position plays an integral role in the conference proceedings. The chair has the authority to determine the logistics of the conference such as the time and location of the meetings (Tiefer 1989). While at first glance this may seem a trivial power (perhaps even burdensome), the chair, in her or his capacity to schedule conferences, can potentially influence the conference outcome. Conference chairs may schedule conferences for times and locations that are inconvenient to members that threaten certain agreements. Chairs have even been known to change the time or location of a meeting with short notice to hinder the participation of dissident conferees (Longley and Oleszek 1989).

Once in conference, the chair has substantial agenda-setting power over which provisions are addressed in a given meeting and the order in which those provisions are considered. By way of this agenda-setting prerogative, the chair may structure meetings according to a variety of considerations, such as informal negotiations outside of conference and the members in attendance. Moreover, the chair also "sets the pace of conference bargaining, and recommends tentative agreements" (Tiefer 1989, 806). Examples abound of conference chairs who have manipulated the duration of or spacing between meetings in effort to influence outcomes.[18] And, depending upon the bargaining structure agreed to in conference, the right to propose agreements may carry substantial weight. All of these powers come in addition to the considerable influence this member is likely to already have among the members of her or his delegation, by means of holding a leadership role in the standing committee (e.g., chair of committee, chair of subcommittee, or senior member).

Only one formal rule governs the organization of the conference negotiations. According to House and Senate rules, conference committees are required to hold meetings in open sessions,[19] unless action has been taken to allow for particular meetings to be closed to the public.[20] This rule, adopted in both chambers in 1975 as part of the sunshine rules (discussed in more detail in chapter 1), attempted to lift the veil of secrecy surrounding conference committee proceedings. In reality, however, much of the inner workings of conference bargaining remain out of view of the public eye (Longley and Oleszek 1989). Groups of conferees, for example, can always meet privately to discuss deals, and, in so doing, exclude other conferees from the negotiations. This, according to members, has been the growing trend in modern conference committees. For example, Democrats have accused Republican conferees of locking them out of conference negotiations, particularly on important measures (Allen and Cochran 2003).

The Democrats' dissatisfaction is not the first time members of Congress have expressed discontent with conference practices, nor is it likely to be the last. A primary reason for this is the utter lack of structure in conference bargaining. In negotiating a resolution, conferees usually operate without formal rules on most procedural matters (Bach 2001). Instead, these details are left to the conferees to decide.

In theory, however, the conferees are not completely free to do as they please. Rather, the decisions made in conference are constrained by chamber rules. Both the House and Senate have rules that limit conferees to considering only the matters in disagreement between the versions of the bill. In other words, conferees are bound by the "scope" of House-Senate differences – they are not intended to modify provisions that have been agreed to by both chambers or introduce language that has not appeared in at least one of the versions.[21] To use a simple quantitative example, when the House and Senate recommend different spending levels, conferees are expected to arrive at a compromise within the limits of these figures (Longley and Oleszek 1989).

However, conferees are given a tremendous amount of flexibility within these constraints. For one, it is often difficult to define the scope of the disagreement. While this may (at least on the surface) appear straight-forward for purely quantitative measures, such as in the example above, it is far more complicated for measures with qualitative components. In addition, conferees are given considerable legislative autonomy in circumstances when one chamber passes the other chamber's bill with an amendment in the nature of a substitute (Longley and Oleszek 1989). This commonly used device replaces the text of the original bill with entirely new language. Since chamber rules dictate that conferees are limited to considering only those provisions in disagreement, an amendment in the nature of a substitute essentially frees all of the language to be modified in conference. Conferees may then propose an entirely new version of the bill, provided that the modifications are germane (Bach 2001).[22]

Although conferees are afforded considerable latitude within the chamber rules, conferees do not always adhere to those rules. Quite frequently conferees violate the formal constraints placed on their negotiations (Oleszek et al. 2016). It is not, for instance, uncommon for conferees to insert provisions on sections not committed to them or to strike from the legislation language agreed to by both chambers. A conference agreement that violates chamber rules in this fashion is subject to a point of order. However, conference agreements rarely encounter points of order, even when they overtly overstep their bounds (Vander Wielen 2006).

Once the conferees reach an agreement, a document, referred to as the conference report, is prepared. It contains the conference committee's proposal for resolving the differences between the House and Senate versions, in formal legislative language. In addition to the conference report, the conferees from both chambers prepare a joint explanatory statement, which describes the agreement in greater detail, perhaps even offering additional information and analysis (Longley and Oleszek 1989). Of particular importance to the conference report and joint explanatory statement are conferee signatures. A majority of each chamber's delegation must sign both documents before the conference report can go back to the chambers for final consideration. House conferees with limited authority are only permitted to sign the section of the conference report within their jurisdiction. The signatures, therefore, represent a vote in favor of the conference agreement. It is significant that both the House and Senate delegations must independently arrive at a majority. This prevents one chamber from holding disproportionate power on the conference committee by means of appointing a larger delegation.

Conference committees need not, however, result in an agreement, as conferees are not required to file a conference report. A complete failure to achieve any consensus is rare. It is also possible for conference committees to result in partial agreements.[23] Conferees, for example, may choose to return some proposed amendments separately from the conference report.

This is often the case when conferees wish to resolve some House-Senate differences with proposals that exceed their authority, such as reaching outside the scope of differences (Rybicki 2015; Longley and Oleszek 1989). The conferees choose to send these proposals, called amendments in technical disagreement, independently of the conference report so as to avoid drawing points of order against the report. Although the name is misleading, these proposals are generally supported by the conferees from both chambers, and are brought to the floor accordingly.[24] Once the chambers have approved the partial conference report, they consider each amendment in disagreement upon the conferees' recommendation for disposing of it (Bach 2001). Typically these amendments are approved without objection or lengthy discussion (Longley and Oleszek 1989).[25]

If conferees are unable to resolve certain matters in disagreement, they may choose to send to the chambers a partial report accompanied by amendments in true disagreement. In doing this, members are acknowledging an impasse in the negotiations, but do not wish to threaten those provisions that had been agreed to. In short, when amendments in true disagreement are sent to the chambers, the responsibility for reconciling these differences is again turned over to the parent bodies.

Post-Conference Stage

Upon the completion of the conference negotiations, the conferees file a report and joint explanatory statement that return to the chambers for final consideration. As earlier discussed, a norm dictates that the chamber that agreed to conference will act first in the consideration of the conference report. This is not, however, a rigid practice, and the ordering can be changed by the approval of the conferees.

There are some important differences between the House and Senate in taking up the conference report. In the House, as in the Senate, the conference report is privileged and may be brought to the floor with relative ease. Once the bill has been brought to the floor of the House,[26] points of order must be made immediately.[27] The conference manager may request that all points of order be waived under unanimous consent. If, however, a conference manager anticipates that a point of order will be raised against the conference report, she or he may try, instead, to bring the conference report to the floor under suspension of rules. Suspension of rules is infrequently used since its success demands two-thirds support. Members may turn to its use, though, if other methods for avoiding points of order are unattainable (Longley and Oleszek 1989). Alternatively, a conference manager may seek a special rule from the Rules Committee that waives points of order against the conference report. Obtaining a special rule, of course, requires the support of a majority of members seated on the Rules Committee. If the conference manager seeks to protect the conference report from points of order by special rule, opponents may regain the ability to issue a point of order if they manage to defeat the previous question (Tiefer 1989).

If the House is the first to act on the conference report, a successful point of order raised against the report has the same effect as a vote to recommit. The sustained point of order returns the conference report to the conference committee where it will likely reconsider the provisions that drew the criticism, time permitting. Conversely, if the House is the second acting chamber and a successful point of order is raised against the report, the conference report is rejected (Tiefer 1989).

However, if there is no point of order raised against the conference report, or the conference manager has secured a means of waiving all points of order, the House proceeds to debate the conference report under the one-hour rule. Each party is allotted half of the time to speak, unless both the majority and minority floor managers support the conference report. In such circumstances, a 1985 addition to House Rule XXII permits an opponent of the report to claim one-third of the time for debate (Longley and Oleszek 1989; Tiefer 1989).[28] At the conclusion of the debate, the House then votes to order the previous question and end any further debate. The House is now prepared to vote on the conference report.

In the Senate, the conference manager typically brings the conference report to the floor by unanimous consent (Longley and Oleszek 1989). If, however, there is an objection to the request for unanimous consent, the motion to consider is privileged and nondebatable. The conference manager will then offer the motion, which prompts a vote requiring simple majority support to bring the report to the floor. Historically, a unique opportunity for obstruction existed in the Senate at this stage in the consideration of the conference report. Following the request to consider the report, either by unanimous consent or motion, but before it was agreed to, any Senator was allowed to request that the conference report be read in full (ibid.). Unlike the House, which has means of waiving this step, the Senate had no rule for avoiding the reading (Tiefer 1989). When time was limited and a conference report lengthy, this request effectively killed legislation. Such was the case for the Clean Air Act of 1976 (Longley and Oleszek 1989; Tiefer 1989). The Senate, however, eliminated this requirement in 2000 (Oleszek et al. 2016).

If the conference manager is successful in bringing the conference report to the floor, senators may raise points of order at any time (Tiefer 1989). This differs from House procedures, which prohibit House members from raising points of order beyond their initial disposing. There are, likewise, noteworthy differences between the chambers in terms of the implications of points of order for conference reports. A successful point of order against a conference report for exceeding the scope of House-Senate differences or directing new spending has the effect of striking the offending language from the report. When such a point of order is sustained, the Senate can move to send the remaining language of the conference report (less the stricken text) to the House in the form of an amendment. In practice, however, objections in the form of points of order are uncommon. Rather, the Senate grants conferees considerable autonomy to shape legislation in conference committee. And, traditionally, the chamber does not question the decisions of conferees, for fear of compromising the integrity of those involved in conference negotiations. Moreover, it is not uncommon for the Senate to overturn the rulings of the presiding officer (Longley and Oleszek 1989).

In addition to points of order, senators may at any time offer additional motions that are not permitted by the House. These additional means of disposing of the conference report include motions to postpone, refer, and table. Each has the effect of removing the conference report from immediate consideration. However, use of these motions is exceedingly rare (Longley and Oleszek 1989).

Perhaps the most important difference between House and Senate procedure in the post-conference stage is that once the conference report has been brought to the floor in the Senate, Senate rules do not restrict debate. Senators in opposition to the conference report may, then, wage a filibuster against it. Unlimited speech can lead to the demise of the legislation, or may prompt the chambers to reconsider the conference agreement. For example, in early 2006, following a successful filibuster against the Patriot Act reauthorization conference report, Republican leaders were forced to return to the negotiation table to appease dissenting senators.

Debate can, however, be limited if bill supporters can muster 60 votes to invoke cloture. In practice, filibusters on conference reports are highly uncommon, and debate is often limited by a unanimous consent agreement negotiated by the leaders of both parties.[29] Once debate on the conference report has been concluded, by means of cloture, unanimous consent, or simply no demand for extended debate, the Senate is now prepared to vote on the conference report.

Throughout this process, neither chamber is permitted to amend the conference report.[30] Therefore, when the conference report reaches the final stage of consideration in the House and Senate, both chambers are restricted to actions that do not alter the content of the conference agreement. This practice gives conferees a tremendous amount of leeway in the negotiation process, since rank-and-file members are often reluctant to reject a conference report that contains more favorable than unfavorable provisions (given the considerable demands on time associated with legislating). However, restricting the chambers' ability to offer amendments on the conference report facilitates resolution. If the chambers were allowed to offer amendments to the report, an agreement might never be reached.

The first chamber to vote on the conference report may accept the report, reject it, or recommit the report to conference. A successful motion to recommit the report to the conference committee may lead to revisions in the conference agreement, or may kill the bill if time does not permit the conference to renegotiate a resolution (Tiefer 1989). Opponents have the ability to recommit the report to the conference committee with instructions. Although a motion to recommit with instructions is nonbinding, it provides opponents with a means of articulating the reasons why the bill was recommitted. If, however, the first acting chamber accepts the report, the conference is dissolved and the report proceeds to the other chamber for consideration. The second chamber has only two options for acting on the conference report—accept or reject. Technically, if the second chamber rejects the conference report, it may request a second conference to be held upon the first chamber's approval. In the nineteenth century, it was not uncommon for the second acting chamber to do this. The growing demands on members' time, however, have rendered this practice largely obsolete (ibid.).

If both chambers agree to the conference report, the bill is enrolled and sent to the president to be signed or vetoed. For partial conference reports, however, the chambers must not only approve the report but also dispose of the amendments in a similar fashion (Bach 2001). Despite passage of the partial conference report, the bill remains incomplete until all amendments have been agreed upon.

In considering a partial conference report with amendments, the first acting chamber begins debate and votes on the report. Similar to a full conference report, the partial conference report is not amendable by the chamber. Upon passing the report, the chamber takes up the amendments that accompanied the partial conference report. In so doing, the clerk reads one of the amendments, and the floor manager offers a motion to dispose of it. The floor is then open to other motions and votes are taken in preferential order. At this stage, House rules give priority to those motions that promote agreement between the chambers rather than perfect the measure.[31] The chamber disposes of all amendments in this manner. After having passed the partial conference report and disposed of all amendments, the other chamber engages in the same process. The bill is ready to be enrolled and presented to the president if both chambers approve the report and take the same course of action in disposing of the amendments.[32]

A slightly modified post-conference process is possible under circumstances in which the conference report contains nongermane Senate amendments. Rules changes adopted in the 1970s authorize the House to effectively remove nongermane Senate amendments from a conference report without rejecting the report in its entirety (Tiefer 1989). Conference reports containing Senate amendments that violate House germaneness requirements are subject to a point of order, provided that prior action has not been taken to waive such objections. If the Speaker sustains a point of order of this nature against a conference report, a member, pursuant to Rule XXII,[33] can move to reject the nongermane provision. Once this motion has been offered, House rules permit 40 minutes of debate to be evenly divided between those who support and oppose the motion. At the conclusion of debate, the House votes on the motion to reject. If the House defeats the motion, it keeps the Senate's nongermane amendment in place (ibid.). Conversely, if the House agrees to the motion, the conference report is technically rejected. However, members are afforded the opportunity to offer a motion that, if agreed to, sends all portions of the conference report that were not rejected back to the Senate. Formally, this is a motion to recede and concur in the Senate amendment with an amendment that consists of the remaining provisions of the conference report (Bach 2001).[34] By doing so, the House resorts to the exchange of amendments between the chambers.

Part B. The Bias from Post-Passage Politics: Additional Materials

In chapter 3, we offered an overview of the median liberal-conservative ideology scores for single-committee conference delegations in both chambers. Here, we provide similar figures for multi-committee conferences in figures B.1 and B.2. The general pattern for multi-committee delegations is very similar to the single-committee conferences that were discussed in chapter 3.

Results of the difference-of-means tests fully support the empirical claims from tables 3.2 and 3.3. It is clear that a significant portion of (sub) conferences have their medians located on the majority party side of the parent chamber median. We further examine whether or not this pattern of bias is of a meaningful magnitude in tables B.1 and B.2. In the House, the pro-majority bias is statistically significant in most Congresses for both single-committee conferences and subconferences with two types of conferees. While there is some evidence of statistically meaningful bias in the Senate, it is less consistent, particularly for conferences with both general- and limited-purpose conferees.

The difference-of-means tests comparing limited-purpose subconferences to both general-purpose and pooled subconferences are shown in tables B.3 and B.4. The *t*-statistic values indicate that the policy distance between limited-purpose conferees and both general-purpose conferees and all members with voting rights on the (sub)conference are, in many Congresses, greater than would be expected by chance.

Last, we report the full multivariate linear regression results that were previously summarized in table 3.7 of chapter 3. In table B.5, we have two models for the two types of House conferences (single-committee conferences and subconferences from multi-committee conferences). In table B.6, we have the model for Senate conferences, and all Senate conferences and House subconferences, pooled.

Part C. A Matching Analysis of the
Decline of Conference Committees

We supplement the analysis in chapter 4 with a bill-level examination of the use of conference across public laws between the 88th and 111th Congresses (1963–2010). In particular, we explore whether there was a statistically discernible disjuncture in the use of conference following the second wave of change in post-passage politics (that is, the post-1994 period discussed in the text). We proceed in two stages, by examining (1) whether there was a meaningful decline in the likelihood of using conference across all bills, and (2) whether the decline in the use of conference was more pronounced in the fiscal policy domain than it was in agriculture and defense.

A challenge in evaluating the effects of intensifying partisan conflict on

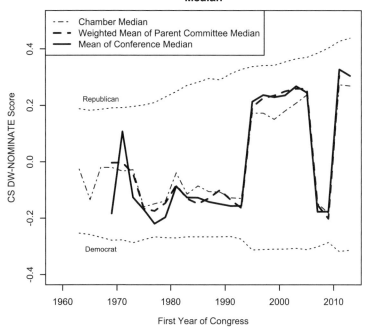

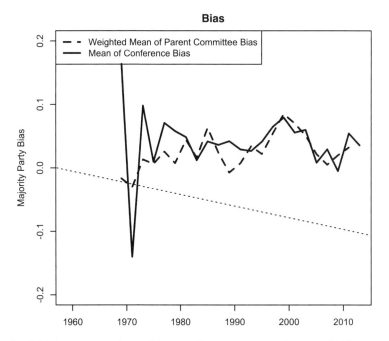

Fig. B.1. Majority party bias in House multi-committee conferences, 1963–2014. (Compiled by the authors from *Calendars of the United States House of Representatives and History of Legislation, Final Edition*, 88th Congress–113th Congress [for the conference membership], Charles Stewart website (http://web.mit.edu/17.251/www/data_page.html) [for standing committee membership], and voteview.org [for CS DW-NOMINATE scores].)

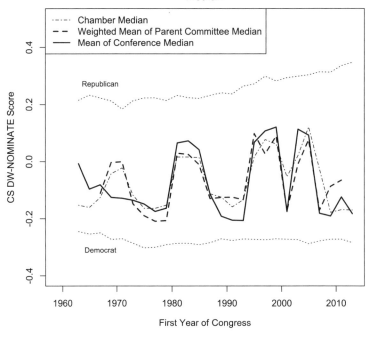

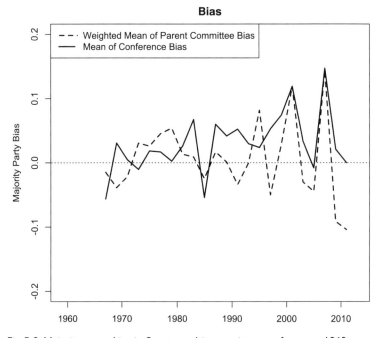

Fig. B.2. Majority party bias in Senate multi-committee conferences, 1963–2014. (Compiled by the authors from *Calendars of the United States House of Representatives and History of Legislation, Final Edition*, 88th Congress–113th Congress [for the conference membership], Charles Stewart website (http://web.mit.edu/17.251/www/data_page.html) [for standing committee membership], and voteview.org [for CS DW-NOMINATE scores].)

post-passage processes is that partisan conflict affects both the choice of post-passage process and the choices made earlier in the legislative process (going to committee, floor action, the structure of the legislation, and the like) that also influence the choice of post-passage process. In principle, a way to address this challenge is to compare action before and after 1994 for bills that are similar. That is, we begin the analyses by preprocessing the data using matching methods and then estimate models to evaluate the magnitude of change that occurred from the pre-1994 period to the post-1994 period. The preprocessing step offers important statistical advantages to the analysis by imposing greater independence between the treatment (in this case, the post-1994 period) and other key explanatory variables (Ho

TABLE B.1. Difference-of-means test for majority party bias in the House, 1963–2014

Congress	Majority Party	Single-Committee Conference		Subconference with Both General- and Limited-Purpose Conferees	
		Congress	Period	Congress	Period
88	Democratic	1.27		n.a.	
89	Democratic	−6.83		n.a.	
90	Democratic	2.88*		n.a.	
91	Democratic	5.49*	6.38*	2.46*	1.22
92	Democratic	3.36*		n.a.	
93	Democratic	7.35*		1.18	
94	Democratic	3.58*		0.19	
95	Democratic	5.15*		4.27*	
96	Democratic	2.61*		4.57*	
97	Democratic	8.20*		3.75*	
98	Democratic	6.57*		0.80	
99	Democratic	5.52*	15.98*	4.77*	13.50*
100	Democratic	5.67*		5.66*	
101	Democratic	7.06*		6.99*	
102	Democratic	4.56*		5.08*	
103	Democratic	10.23*		4.58*	
104	Republican	4.93*		3.98*	
105	Republican	11.03*		8.44*	
106	Republican	10.58*	14.04*	8.48*	12.62*
107	Republican	3.01*		5.25*	
108	Republican	4.68*		9.10*	
109	Republican	4.01*		0.94	
110	Democratic	5.61*	5.09*	4.59*	3.20*
111	Democratic	2.30*		−0.41	
112	Republican	0.38	1.28	11.53*	10.47*
113	Republican	1.31		1.89*	

Note: t-statistics are shown for H_0: bias = 0; whenever the t-test is not performed (# cases < 2), it is denoted as n.a. (not applicable); *$p < 0.05$ (one-tailed test).

et al. 2007). In particular, we match on the basis of characteristics of legislation that plausibly influence the use of conference. For instance, there is a long-standing observation that important measures go to conference. If the number of important measures changes, it might well account for the change in post-passage processes independently of changes in partisan conflict.

Changes in Conference—All Public Laws

We begin by looking at the post-passage methods used for all public laws enacted between the 88th and 111th Congresses (1963–2010). As noted in the text, we theorize that the second wave of change, which ushered

TABLE B.2. Difference-of-means test for majority party bias in the Senate, 1963–2014

Congress	Majority Party	Single-Committee Conference		Conference with Both General- and Limited-Purpose Conferees	
		Congress	Period	Congress	Period
88	Democratic	−8.83		n.a.	
89	Democratic	−5.15		n.a.	
90	Democratic	−3.81		−1.57	
91	Democratic	7.59*		0.60	
92	Democratic	10.00*	0.88	0.19	−0.45
93	Democratic	1.86*		−0.28	
94	Democratic	−1.65		0.97	
95	Democratic	1.33		0.73	
96	Democratic	1.15		0.17	
97	Republican	4.72*		1.11	
98	Republican	4.97*	7.11*	1.66	0.35
99	Republican	2.41*		−1.91	
100	Democratic	0.07		3.68*	
101	Democratic	5.27*		2.49*	
102	Democratic	4.36*	7.47*	2.14*	4.79*
103	Democratic	6.92*		0.65	
104	Republican	4.31*		1.43	
105	Republican	1.67*	5.73*	1.45	3.03*
106	Republican	4.26*		2.38*	
107	Democratic	6.03*	6.03*	n.a.	
108	Republican	4.81*		0.65	
109	Republican	−1.30	2.70*	−0.25	0.31
110	Democratic	9.26*		n.a.	
111	Democratic	0.78	4.38*	7.00*	1.40
112	Democratic	−1.64		n.a.	
113	Republican	−0.57	−0.57	n.a.	

Note: t-statistics are shown for H_0: bias = 0; whenever the t-test is not performed (# cases < 2), it is denoted as n.a. (not applicable); *$p < 0.05$ (one-tailed test).

in historically high levels of partisanship, led to a decline in the use of conference. A brief examination of the data demonstrates the need for preprocessing. Figure C.1, for instance, shows the considerable disparity in distributions of legislative importance across the pre- and post-1994 eras, using our categorical measure of importance developed in the text: legislation is considered to be "highly important" if the length in column lines in *CQ Almanac* is greater than its median value (125 lines), "somewhat important" if the bill is discussed in *CQ Almanac* but under the median for length of coverage, and "least important" if the bill is not covered in *CQ Almanac*. The differences in these distributions are substantively and statistically meaningful, and furthermore we know that legislative importance is a critical determinant of the use of conference.

Our aim is to mitigate these discrepancies in legislation across the two periods in our analysis. We do this by matching legislation across the two

TABLE B.3. Difference-of-means test for limited-purpose subconference bias in the House multi-committee conferences, 1971–2014

Congress	Majority Party	Against General-Purpose Subconference		Against All Subconference	
		Congress	Period	Congress	Period
92	Democratic	n.a.		n.a.	
93	Democratic	n.a.	2.61*	1.00	1.60
94	Democratic	n.a.		n.a.	
95	Democratic	0.02		0.02	
96	Democratic	−1.21		−0.49	
97	Democratic	1.73*		4.44*	
98	Democratic	−0.32		0.41	
99	Democratic	2.42*	0.92	0.77	0.82
100	Democratic	2.09*		2.10*	
101	Democratic	−2.17		−1.64	
102	Democratic	0.31		−0.51	
103	Democratic	−3.70		−0.23	
104	Republican	2.62*		2.01*	
105	Republican	0.78		0.19	
106	Republican	2.49*	4.13*	1.16	3.24*
107	Republican	−1.92		−0.64	
108	Republican	2.38*		1.73*	
109	Republican	4.97*		4.78*	
110	Democratic	5.07*	4.41*	4.82*	4.12*
111	Democratic	1.07		1.07	
112	Republican	2.08*	2.28*	−0.32	0.19
113	Republican	1.50		1.39	

Note: *t*-statistics are shown for H_0: bias = 0; whenever the t-test is not performed (# cases < 2), it is denoted as n.a. (not applicable); $*p < 0.05$ (one-tailed test).

periods on the basis of observable covariates, including the substantive focus of the legislation, its legislative importance, and whether the legislation has fiscal implications. To capture the substantive focus of the legislation, we use the major issue coding provided by the Policy Agendas Project. We discussed our measure of legislative importance above. Finally, we measure fiscal bills as those that originated in the appropriations, budget, or tax committees of either chamber. We account for fiscal bills since the major topic codes do not necessarily capture this information, and we believe that this is an important, independent dimension affecting the use of conference.

We perform the matching procedure using the R package MatchIt (Ho et al. 2011). We also confirm these and subsequent results using the R package OptMatch (Hansen et al. 2016). We utilize a nearest neighbor matching method that seeks to minimize the global distance across all matched pairs, and we note that alternative propensity score methods arrive at sub-

TABLE B.4. Difference-of-means test for limited-purpose subconference bias in the Senate multi-committee conferences, 1973–2014

Congress	Majority Party	Against General-Purpose Subconference		Against All Subconference	
		Congress	Period	Congress	Period
93	Democratic	n.a.		n.a.	
94	Democratic	n.a.	−3.25	n.a.	−2.05
95	Democratic	−1.05		−0.79	
96	Democratic	−3.11		−1.88	
97	Republican	−1.15		0.30	
98	Republican	−0.17	−1.87	0.35	1.06
99	Republican	−1.71		1.43	
100	Democratic	−0.68		−1.58	
101	Democratic	−2.44		−0.12	
102	Democratic	−0.45	−1.92	0.22	−1.10
103	Democratic	n.a.		n.a.	
104	Republican	−0.67		3.39*	
105	Republican	0.58	0.88	0.35	2.39*
106	Republican	2.23*		0.79	
107	Democratic	n.a.		n.a.	
108	Republican	n.a.	−0.47	n.a.	−0.67
109	Republican	−0.73		−0.98	
110	Democratic	−5.84		−5.84	
111	Democratic	n.a.	−5.84	n.a.	−5.84
112	Democratic	n.a.		n.a.	
113	Republican	n.a.		n.a.	

Note: t-statistics are shown for H_0: bias = 0; whenever the t-test is not performed (# cases < 2), it is denoted as n.a. (not applicable); *$p < 0.05$ (one-tailed test).

TABLE B.5. Multivariate linear model of conference bias (I)

	House	
	Single-Committee Conference	Multi-Committee Conference
Conference size	−0.06 (−0.77)	−0.04* (−7.01)
General–purpose parent committee bias	0.66* (16.65)	0.22* (6.93)
Limited–purpose parent committee bias		0.07* (2.52)
General–purpose parent committee type		
- Constituency committee (omitted)	—	—
- Policy committee	0.06* (7.09)	0.04* (5.93)
- Prestige committee	−0.00 (−0.11)	0.03* (2.43)
Limited-purpose parent committee type		
- Constituency committee (omitted)		—
- Policy committee		0.01† (1.73)
- Prestige committee		0.01 (0.93)
Important bill		
- Least important (omitted)	—	—
- Somewhat important	0.03* (3.45)	−0.01 (−0.43)
- Highly important	0.03* (3.31)	−0.02† (−1.84)
Partisan bill		
- No roll call vote (omitted)	—	—
- Roll call but no party vote	(1.48)	−0.03* (−2.68)
- Party vote	0.03* (3.86)	−0.01 (−1.25)
Policy domain		
- Appropriations	−0.00 (−0.15)	−0.02 (−0.94)
- Budget	−0.01 (−0.20)	−0.01 (−1.09)
- Tax	−0.04 (−1.71)	0.02 (0.42)
- Others (omitted)	—	—
Congress–level partisan environment		
- Interparty distance	0.45* (2.01)	−0.74* (−3.80)
- Majority party homogeneity	−0.02† (−1.89)	0.02* (2.89)
- Majority party size	−0.36* (−4.11)	−0.25† (−1.88)
Period		
- First wave (95th-103rd)	0.01 (1.29)	0.06* (2.61)
- Second wave (104th-112th)	−0.01 (−0.40)	0.07* (2.50)
Constant	0.09 (0.95)	0.42* (3.67)
N	1,559	984
F–statistic	50.19*	24.51*
R^2	0.34	0.33

Note: Unit of analysis is the voting unit of each chamber's conference delegations; dependent variable is the conference bias toward the majority party; whenever categorical variables are used, the omitted baseline category is noted; coefficients are shown with t-values in parenthesis. $*p < 0.05$, $†p < 0.10$.

stantively similar results. This approach is quite successful in achieving balance in legislation across the two periods, as shown in table C.1.

We suppress the statistics for the twenty categories of the major topic variable to conserve space; however, we note that statistically meaningful differences in distributions of categories across the treated and control groups in the unmatched data were nearly entirely eliminated in the matched data (only one category exhibits a statistically significant difference across the treated and control groups in the matched data as compared to eleven categories that had statistically significant differences in

TABLE B.6. Multivariate linear model of conference bias (2)

	Senate	House and Senate Pooled
Chamber		
- House *(omitted)*	—	
- Senate		−0.03* (−8.29)
Conference size	−0.17* (−3.95)	−0.06* (−11.05)
General-purpose parent committee bias	0.74* (29.22)	0.59* (32.76)
General-purpose parent committee type		
- Constituency committee *(omitted)*	—	—
- Policy committee	0.02* (2.34)	0.03* (6.27)
- Prestige committee	−0.02* (−2.28)	−0.02* (−2.93)
Important bill		
- Least important *(omitted)*	—	—
- Somewhat important	−0.00 (−0.57)	0.01* (2.31)
- Highly important	−0.01 (−1.18)	0.01 (1.28)
Partisan bill		
- No roll call vote *(omitted)*	—	—
- Roll call but no party vote	−0.02* (−2.96)	−0.00 (−0.92)
- Party vote	−0.00 (−0.47)	0.01 (2.03)
Policy domain		
- Appropriations	0.01 (0.81)	0.00 (0.56)
- Budget	0.03 (1.50)	0.02* (2.74)
- Tax	−0.06* (−3.20)	−0.05* (−3.61)
- Others *(omitted)*	—	—
Congress-level partisan environment		
- Interparty distance	0.10 (0.77)	−0.11* (−2.14)
- Majority party homogeneity	0.00 (0.76)	−0.00 (0.55)
- Majority party size	−0.84* (−13.56)	−0.56* (−14.33)
Period		
- First wave (95th-103rd)	−0.01 (−1.01)	0.03* (6.79)
- Second wave (104th-112th)	0.00 (0.23)	0.01* (2.43)
Constant	0.47* (7.03)	0.43* (11.65)
N	1,830	4,408
F-statistic	121.12*	146.06*
R^2	0.52	0.36

Note: Unit of analysis is the voting unit of each chamber's conference delegations; dependent variable is the conference bias toward the majority party; whenever categorical variables are used, the omitted baseline category is noted; coefficients are shown with *t*-values in parenthesis. *$p < 0.05$, † $p < 0.10$.

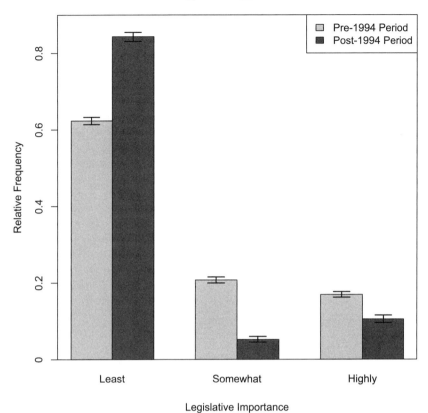

Fig. C.1. Distribution of legislative importance, pre- and post-1994 periods

TABLE C.1. Nearest neighbor matching result

	Unmatched Data			Matched Data		
	Treated Mean	Control Mean	Difference	Treated Mean	Control Mean	Difference
Importance	0.2618	0.5461	−0.2842*	0.2618	0.2630	−0.0011
Fiscal	0.0536	0.0715	−0.0179*	0.0536	0.0465	0.0071
Propensity Score Distance	0.3013	0.2434	0.0580*	0.3013	0.3009	0.0004

Note: $^*p < 0.05$ for the difference-in-means test.

the unmatched data). In addition, the relatively sizable differences across the treated and control groups for the importance and fiscal variables before matching are all but nullified in the matched data. The resulting difference in the propensity score for the matched data is negligible, and there is marked improvement in the comparability of the propensity score distributions across the treated and control groups after matching (see

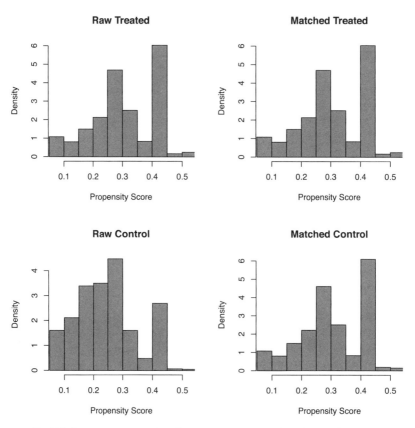

Fig. C.2. Propensity score distributions across treated and control groups before and after matching

figure C.2). To attain this level of balancing, we discarded 6,559 control observations, and found 3,506 matched bills (n = 7,012).

We proceed to use these matched data in a parametric analysis examining changes in the use of conference. This approach to parametric modeling is more robust and less susceptible to bias than an approach that skips the preprocessing stage described above (Ho et al. 2007). We estimate a logistic regression model in which our dependent variable measuring whether the given bill was resolved in conference is a function of an indicator variable for treated bills (i.e., occurring in the post-1994 period), legislative importance, and an indicator variable for fiscal bills. As expected, the treatment variable is negative and statistically significant, indicating a reduction in the use of conference in the post-1994 period. In order to better understand the implications of this result, we simulate the treatment effect. The results of this simulation can be found in table C.2. Importantly, we find a statistically discernible drop in use of conference of approximately 1.3 percentage points for a typical bill. We now turn to an analysis that offers a more comprehensive account of the moderating effect that issue domain has on this relationship.

Changes in Conference—Dependence on Policy Domain

While the results in the above analysis point to a statistically meaningful decline in the use of conference across all bills, we theorize that this decline will be more pronounced in the fiscal domain than it is in the agriculture or defense domains, which have been associated with less partisan pressure and fewer institutional changes across time. To examine this proposition in more detail, we restrict our attention to only those bills within the fiscal, agriculture, or defense domains. We limit our public law dataset to these bills using our fiscal variable, described above, in conjunction with the major topic codes for agriculture and defense. The resulting dataset consists of 2,403 bills.

As in the preceding analysis, we first preprocess the bills using the same matching technique. The results of this matching strategy are presented in table C.3. Naturally, considering the restrictions made to the data at the outset, the unevenness in the distributions across the treated and control groups is less dramatic than we saw in the above analysis. Nonetheless, we are again successful in improving the balance across groups, and thus achieving a more accurate comparison of legislation across time. Even for the importance variable, which did not exhibit a statistically significant difference between the treated and control groups in the unmatched data, we were able to generate a 28.6 percent improvement in balance. Moreover, the statistically significant difference in the fiscal variable is entirely erased. As before, we suppress the statistics for the now-eighteen categories of the major topic variable to conserve space, but have eliminated all statistical differences that were present within categories in the unmatched data

TABLE C.2. Simulation result for treatment effect

	Pre-1994 Period	Post-1994 Period	Difference
Estimate	0.0262	0.0133	−0.0130
95% Confidence Interval	[0.0212, 0.0320]	[0.0103, 0.0172]	[−0.0183, −0.0083]
p-value	<0.001	<0.001	<0.001

(two categories exhibited statistical differences in the unmatched data). Note that there remains variation in the major topic variable despite the restrictions made to the dataset because fiscal bills address myriad topics. The resulting difference in the propensity score for the matched data is trivial. The matching discarded 1,579 control observations, and found 412 matched bills (n = 824).

To test the central proposition—that the changes in the use of conference are more pronounced in the fiscal policy domain than in the agriculture or defense domains—we implement a difference-in-difference (DID) analysis on the matched data. We do this simply by adding an interaction term between the treatment variable and the fiscal indicator to the logistic regression model used in the above analysis. The model is shown in Equation (C-1) below, where δ is the DID estimator. Since the model is nonlinear, making direct interpretation difficult, and the DID estimator is an interaction, complicating the determination of statistical significance, we simulate the difference in treatment effects across the two policy domains.

$$Conf = \alpha + \beta * Importance + \gamma * Fiscal + \tau * Treatment$$
$$+ \delta * (Fiscal * Treatment) + \varepsilon \qquad\qquad \text{C-1}$$

The results of the simulation are shown in table C.4, where we present the treatment effects for both of the policy domains as well as the DID

TABLE C.3. Nearest neighbor matching result, for fiscal, agriculture, and defense bills only

	Unmatched Data			Matched Data		
	Treated Mean	Control Mean	Difference	Treated Mean	Control Mean	Difference
Importance	0.8786	0.8548	0.0238	0.8786	0.8617	0.0170
Fiscal	0.4563	0.3616	0.0947*	0.4563	0.4563	0.0000
Propensity Score Distance	0.1891	0.1678	0.0213*	0.1891	0.1843	0.0048

Note: *p < 0.05 for the difference-in-means test.

TABLE C.4. Simulation result for treatment effect, for fiscal, agriculture, and defense bills only

	Treatment Effect (Agriculture/ Defense)	Treatment Effect (Fiscal)	DID Estimator (Fiscal-Ag/Def)
Estimate	0.0096	−0.1401	−0.1498
95% Confidence Interval	[−0.0484, 0.0687]	[−0.2761, −0.0017]	[−0.2980, −0.0018]
p-value	0.7444	0.0463	0.0488

estimator, calculated as: $(E[Y \mid T = 1, F = 1] - E[Y \mid T = 0, F = 1]) - (E[Y \mid T = 1, F = 0] - E[Y \mid T = 0, F = 0])$. Interestingly, we find no statistically meaningful treatment effect for agriculture and defense bills. That is, there is no measurable change in the use of conference across time within this policy domain. However, as expected, we observe a marked, and statistically meaningful, drop in the use of conference among fiscal bills. Fiscal bills in the post-1994 period are approximately 14 percentage points less likely to go to conference than they were in the previous period. Not surprisingly, the DID estimator points to a statistically significant difference in the treatment effects across these policy domains (of approximately 15 percentage points).

In sum, the first stage of this analysis shows an effect of the post-1994 period on the use of conference across all bills. Because we aggregate in this fashion, it is not entirely surprising that the decline, while statistically meaningful, is relatively small in magnitude. However, the second stage of the analysis shows that the decline is considerable in policy domains most central to partisan politics.

Notes

CHAPTER 1

1. The rules limit the number of times that amendments can be exchanged. The second-acting chamber's amendment to the original measure is the text subject to amendment, and each chamber is then allowed one opportunity to amend the opposing chamber's amendment. However, both chambers can and do waive these limitations on the number of exchanges permitted.

2. Technically speaking there is no written rule precluding the amendment of a conference report. Rather, it is a precedent rooted in *Jefferson's Manual* (Sec. XLVI; 4th Cong., 1st Sess., S. Jour., p. 270).

3. In the appendix, part A, we provide more detailed information on how conference works. While these procedures are critical to the various stages of conference proceedings, our theoretical model does not require an in-depth understanding of these procedural details.

4. The Mayhew list is being updated through 2012 (campuspress.yale.edu/davidmayhew/ datasets-divided-we-govern/, accessed September 12, 2016).

5. See Tsebelis and Money (1997) for another example of a formal model of conference outcomes.

6. To capture the important components of polarization—interparty heterogeneity and intraparty homogeneity—we measure polarization as the ratio of the absolute difference between Republican and Democratic Party medians, and the square root of the average of the variances of the parties, or $|Median_R - Median_D| \div \sqrt{(\sigma_R^2 + \sigma_D^2)/2}$. We also use this measure elsewhere (Vander Wielen and Smith 2011).

7. For a thorough discussion of these reforms, see Deering and Smith (1997).

8. In 1973, Senate Republicans reformed their rules to permit committee members to select their ranking member, and Democrats adopted rules changes in 1975 that provided, at the request of one-fifth of the conference, for a vote on committee chairs (Schickler, McGhee, and Sides 2003).

9. On the developments leading up to the enactment of budget reform in 1974, see Schick (1980, 17–81).

10. Since 1995, Speakers can no longer send a bill jointly to more than one committee.

CHAPTER 2

1. http://housedocs.house.gov/rules/health/111_ahcaa.pdf

2. For a more detailed discussion, see Beth and Rybicki (2003).

3. In January 2007, the House of Representatives adopted a new rule that requires conference committees to be open to all conferees.

4. It also bears notice that the Senate rules limiting a conference report to the scope of the differences between the House and Senate versions of a bill and requiring that a conference report be available online for 48 hours before a floor vote do not apply to amendments between the houses (Beth et al. 2009). It also is noteworthy that Senate Republicans adopted a standing order as a part of a 1996 bill that provides that conference reports are not required to be read. House amendments are not exempt, so a reading of an amendment could consume considerable time.

5. Policy Agendas Project (policyagendas.org, accessed February 18, 2016). The data used were originally collected by Frank R. Baumgartner and Bryan D. Jones, with the support of National Science Foundation grant numbers SBR 9320922 and 0111611, and were distributed through the Department of Government at the University of Texas at Austin. Neither NSF nor the original collectors of the data bear any responsibility for the analysis reported here.

6. Political Institutions and Public Choice Roll-Call Database (cacexplore.org/pipcvotes, accessed February 18, 2016).

7. We utilize the Policy Agendas Project database to identify the standing committee of origin in the House, and then apply Deering and Smith's (1997) standing committees typology to group the standing committees of origin into one of the three mutually exclusive categories they introduce—prestige, policy, or constituency. See Deering and Smith (1997) for a complete list of the committees included in each category.

8. We use 83.5 percent confidence intervals so that we can compare the intervals for overlap as a two-tailed test of statistical significance at the standard type 1 error rate of 5 percent, that is, 95 percent confidence (see, e.g., Goldstein and Healy 1995; Maghsoodloo and Huang 2010).

CHAPTER 3

1. http://voteview.com/dwnomin_joint_house_and_senate.htm

2. If the medians of limited-purpose conferees are, indeed, frequently situated on the majority party side of general-purpose medians, as evidenced by the former analysis, then it stands to reason that combining limited- and general-purpose conferees will shift the collective median toward the majority party median, making it a more demanding test to find statistical significance between limited-purpose conferees and all members with voting rights on the subconference.

3. When in the majority, both parties have given themselves extra seats on the

Rules Committee, where the majority has given itself one more than twice as many seats as the minority (9 to 4) to ensure that absences or political problems are not obstacles to controlling the preparation of special rules for the consideration of major legislation on the floor. There is some compensation for this in giving each party an equal number of seats on the Ethics Committee (before 2011, Standards of Official Conduct). Neither committee is associated with conference committees in most Congresses.

4. We also note that Smith (2007) and Smith and Gamm (2009) argue that the relationship between party polarization and the strength of majority party influence is likely to be stronger in the House than in the Senate. House majority parties may modify the formal powers of their central leader (i.e., the Speaker) through changes in chamber and party rules in a way that strengthens the resources of the central leader. Senate majority parties face a cloture threshold whenever they seek to strengthen their leaders' influence over proceedings. Even changes in internal party rules that strengthen the influence of a central leader in party affairs cannot be readily translated into influence over outcomes on the Senate floor.

CHAPTER 4

1. "Pentagon Money Bill Sticks to 'Summit' Script,'" in *CQ Almanac 1988*, 44th ed. (Washington, DC: Congressional Quarterly, 1989), 651–72; http://library.cqpress.com/cqalmanac/cqal88–1140882

2. http://www.politifact.com/rhode-island/statements/2011/dec/27/barry-hinckley/us-senate-candidate-barry-hinckley-says-nations-ta/ (accessed March 2016).

CHAPTER 5

1. The Senate has rules designed to prevent unwanted "airdropping," provisions that constitute "new matter" or "new directed spending" that are added in conference but not a part of the House or Senate bills.

APPENDIX

1. A third possibility rarely used is a motion to "adhere" to its amendments. This occurs when a chamber returns a bill with a request to change it after the other chamber has already insisted on its amendments. This signifies an unwillingness to compromise on the provisions in dispute (Tiefer 1989).

2. At the time the Rules Committee was dominated by the conservative coalition (Tiefer 1989).

3. House Rule XXII.1 reads: "A motion to disagree to Senate amendments to a House proposition and to request or agree to a conference with the Senate, or a motion to insist on House amendments to a Senate proposition and to request or agree to a conference with the Senate, shall be privileged in the discretion of the Speaker if offered by direction of the primary committee and of all reporting committees that had initial referral of the proposition."

4. The precedence of motions following agreement plays the most substan-

tial role after conference has successfully met (Bach 2001; Longley and Oleszek 1989).

5. The motions, in order of precedence, are to refer to committee, to amend, to agree, or to disagree (Longley and Oleszek 1989).

6. The cloture motion for this single motion to proceed to conference in the Senate is debatable for two hours.

7. *Constitution, Jefferson's Manual,* and *Rules of the House of Representatives,* 113th Congress, 2nd Session, H. Doc. 113–81. 280.

8. The House does have the ability to instruct conferees if they do not report within 25 legislative days after being appointed or within 36 hours after being appointed during the last six days of session (Bach 2001). Such use of the motion to instruct is incredibly rare (Tiefer 1989).

9. The Senate is particularly reluctant to instruct conferees because of "the implied insult to conferees and violation of the value of bicameral compromise" (Longley and Oleszek 1989, 187).

10. House Rule I.11 reads: "The Speaker shall appoint all select, joint, and conference committees ordered by the House. At any time after an original appointment, the Speaker may remove Members, Delegates, or the Resident Commissioner from, or appoint additional Members, Delegates, or the Resident Commissioner to, a select or conference committee. In appointing Members, Delegates, or the Resident Commissioner to conference committees, the Speaker shall appoint no less than a majority who generally supported the House position as determined by the Speaker, shall name those who are primarily responsible for the legislation, and shall, to the fullest extent feasible, include the principal proponents of the major provisions of the bill or resolution passed or adopted by the House."

11. This has proved an important power of the Speaker. In 1998, the fiscal 1998–99 State Department Authorization Bill (H.R. 1757) had encountered some unexpected difficulties in conference. Moderate Republican Jim Leach (R-Iowa), who favored increasing the funds for the United Nations and opposed restriction on family planning funds, put up a fight. Lacking the votes needed to pass the conference report, Speaker Newt Gingrich (R-Georgia) removed Leach and replaced him with conservative Dan Burton (R-Indiana) who proceeded to sign the conference report—ironically, not before having second thoughts himself as to whether or not to give funds to the UN (Cassata 1998).

12. Senate Rule XXIV.1 reads: "In the appointment of the standing committees, or to fill vacancies thereon, the Senate, unless otherwise ordered, shall by resolution appoint the chairman of each such committee and the other members thereof. On demand of any Senator, a separate vote shall be had on the appointment of the chairman of any such committee and on the appointment of the other members thereof. Each such resolution shall be subject to amendment and to division of the question." Senate Rule XXIV.3 continues: "Except as otherwise provided or unless otherwise ordered, all other committees, and the chairmen thereof, shall be appointed in the same manner as standing committees."

13. As such, the chairman and ranking member of the committee or subcommittee (or both) responsible for reporting the bill are almost always appointed to conference (Bach 2001).

14. Traditionally, all conference delegations came from only one committee.

However, with the rise of multiple referrals and omnibus bills, delegations are increasingly composed of more than one committee.

15. Because conferees have varying degrees of authority, the conference is divided into subconferences. A vote is then taken on each subconference and a majority is required for passage of that section.

16. Formally, this is the member listed first on the slate of conferees (Tiefer 1989).

17. Members have gone to lengths to become chair of important conferences, and have fueled unrest in their attempt to do so. There are reports of members artificially creating conferences, by means of adding controversial measures, solely to be chair of the conference negotiations (Oleszek et al. 2016). Tiefer (1989) cites an example in which a standing committee chair attempted to decline the chair of a minor conference in effort to gain the chair of an important upcoming conference.

18. In one such example, Carl Perkins (D-Kentucky), as conference chair on a controversial higher education bill, kept the conference in negotiations for 15 straight hours. An agreement was reported reached because conferees "were numb with exhaustion" (Longley and Oleszek 1989, 202).

19. Technically, House Rule XXII.12.a.1 requires only a single meeting of the conference committee in open session. It reads: "Subject to subparagraph (2), a meeting of each conference committee shall be open to public." Subparagraph (2) refers to the means by which conference can meet in closed session (see note 20).

20. Both chambers have rules that allow for conferences to be closed to the public. The House provision (House Rule XXII.12.a.2) reads: "In open session of the House, a motion that managers on the part of the House be permitted to close to the public a meeting or meetings of their conference committee shall be privileged, shall be decided without debate, and shall be decided by the yeas and nays." The analogous Senate rule (Senate Rule XXVIII.9) reads: "Each conference committee between the Senate and the House of Representatives shall be open to the public except when managers of either the Senate or the House of Representatives in open session determine by a roll call vote of a majority of those managers present, that all or part of the remainder of the meeting on the day of the vote shall be closed to the public." In practice, however, the Senate defers to the House in making this decision (Longley and Oleszek 1989).

21. The House rule (*Constitution, Jefferson's Manual*, and the *Rules of the House of Representatives*, 113th Congress, 2nd Session, H. Doc. 113–181, 929) on this matter reads: "Whenever a disagreement to an amendment has been committed to a conference committee, the managers on the part of the House may propose a substitute that is a germane modification of the matter in disagreement. The introduction of any language presenting specific additional matter not committed to the conference committee by either House does not constitute a germane modification of the matter in disagreement. Moreover, a conference report may not include matter not committed to the conference committee by either House and may not include a modification of specific matter committed to the conference committee by either or both Houses if that modification is beyond the scope of that specific matter as committed to the conference committee." The Senate Rule (XXVIII.3.a) reads: "Conferees shall not insert in their report matter not committed to them by either House, nor shall they strike from the bill matter agreed to by both Houses."

22. That additions be germane is of concern more to the House than the Senate. Tiefer (1989, 814) explains that since the House has a means of waiving the germaneness requirement, and the Senate does not, the Senate has adopted a more lax approach to enforcing the germaneness of conference modifications.

23. This is not true of bills in which one of the chambers passed the bill with an amendment in the nature of a substitute. In this case, the conferees may only report in full agreement or full disagreement, since there is technically only one amendment committed to conference. As a result, there can only be an agreed upon resolution for that amendment or no resolution at all (Longley and Oleszek 1989; Bach 2001).

24. Conferees technically have three options for reporting amendments in technical disagreement: to recede and concur to the other chamber's amendment, to disagree with the amendment, or to recede and concur with a new amendment (Tiefer 1989).

25. Amendments in technical disagreement are particularly common among appropriations bills. The House has stricter germaneness requirements than the Senate, and House conferees are not permitted to agree to certain Senate amendments that provide for unauthorized funds or changes in existing law. As a result, conferees commonly agree to a partial conference report that does not contain such provisions (to insulate it from a point of order), and send the provisions in question separately as amendments in technical disagreement (Longley and Oleszek 1989; Rybicki 2015).

26. In order for the conference report to be considered it must sit for three days after being filed, and must have been printed, along with the joint explanatory statement, in the Congressional Record the day it was filed. In addition, copies of the report and statement must be available to representatives for at least two hours before consideration (Bach 2001).

27. Unanimous consent agreements are frequently worked out in advance by the party leaders.

28. House Rule XXII.8.a.2 reads: "If the floor manager for the majority and the floor manager for the minority both support the conference report or motion, one-third of the time for debate thereon shall be allotted to a Member, Delegate, or Resident Commissioner who opposes the conference report or motion on demand of that Member, Delegate, or Resident Commissioner."

29. Senate Rule XXVIII.3.b requires that if debate on the conference report is limited, time allotted for debate must be evenly divided between the parties.

30. There is no written rule on this in either chamber, but it is a precedent that is rooted in *Jefferson's Manual* (Sec. XLVI; 4th Cong., 1st sess., S. Jour., p. 270). This, however, did not become definitive practice until 1850 (Tiefer 1989).

31. The precedence of motions changes in the House before and after the stage of disagreement has been entered. Preceding disagreement, precedents give priority to motions that perfect the bill, whereas motions that encourage agreement between the chambers are given precedence after disagreement has been established (Longley and Oleszek 1989; Bach 2001). There is, however, a maneuver in the House that allows opposition to an amendment to offer a new amendment. Once a motion to recede and concur has been offered, the opposition may request a division of the motion. The chamber, then, separately considers the motion to recede and the motion to concur. Once the motion to recede has been agreed to,

the House reverts back to the order of precedence preceding the stage of disagreement, allowing for motions perfecting the bill to take priority over those that promote agreement (Longley and Oleszek 1989; Tiefer 1989). The opposition may then offer a motion to concur with an amendment.

32. Typically, for amendments in technical disagreement, the chamber agrees to a motion of the floor manager to recede and concur with an amendment. The amendment, in this case, is the agreement that conferees made that usually is outside the scope of their authority. Amendments in true disagreement may be more cumbersome to come to an agreement on. Often, party leaders in both houses must negotiate an agreement that can be presented to the chambers.

33. House Rule XXII.10.2 reads: "A point of order against nongermane matter is one asserting that a proposition described in subparagraph (1) contains specified matter that would violate clause 7 of rule XVI if it were offered in the House as an amendment to the underlying measure in the form it was passed by the House. (b) If a point of order under paragraph (a) is sustained, a motion that the House reject the nongermane matter identified by the point of order shall be privileged. Such a motion is debatable for 40 minutes, one-half in favor of the motion and one-half in opposition thereto. (c) After disposition of a point of order under paragraph (a) or a motion to reject under paragraph (b), any further points of order under paragraph (a) not covered by a previous point of order, and any consequent motions to reject under paragraph (b), shall be likewise disposed of. (d)(1) If a motion to reject under paragraph (b) is adopted, then after disposition of all points of order under paragraph (a) and any consequent motions to reject under paragraph (b), the conference report or motion, as the case may be, shall be considered as rejected and the matter remaining in disagreement shall be disposed of under subparagraph (2) or (3), as the case may be. (2) After the House has adopted one or more motions to reject nongermane matter contained in a conference report under the preceding provisions of this clause (A) if the conference report accompanied a House measure amended by the Senate, the pending question shall be whether the House shall recede and concur in the Senate amendment with an amendment consisting of so much of the conference report as was not rejected; and (B) if the conference report accompanied a Senate measure amended by the House, the pending question shall be whether the House shall insist further on the House amendment."

34. A member can also offer a motion to insist on the House amendment.

References

Aldrich, John H., and David W. Rohde. 2009. "Congressional Committees in a Continuing Partisan Era." In *Congress Reconsidered, 9th Edition*, ed. Lawrence C. Dodd and Bruce I. Oppenheimer. Washington, DC: CQ Press.

Allen, Jonathan, and John Cochran. 2003. "The Might of the Right." *CQ Weekly* (November 8): 2761–62.

Allison, Stevens. 2004. "Will Conference-Blocking Tactic Come Back to Bite Democrats?" *CQ Weekly* (January 31): 266.

Bach, Stanley. 2001. "Conference Committee and Related Procedures: An Introduction." *Congressional Research Services* (January 17).

Beth, Richard S., Valerie Heitshusen, Bill Heniff, and Elizabeth Rybicki. 2009. "Leadership Tools for Managing the U.S. Senate." Paper presented at the Annual Meeting of the American Political Science Association, Toronto.

Beth, Richard S., and Elizabeth Rybicki. 2003. "Sufficiency of Signatures on Conference Reports." *Congressional Research Service: CRS Report RS21629* (September 30).

Binder, Sarah A., and Frances E. Lee. 2016. "Making Deals in Congress." In *Political Negotiation: A Handbook*, ed. Jane Mansbridge and Cathie Jo Martin, Washington, DC: Brookings.

Black, Duncan. 1948. "On the Rationale of Group Decision-Making." *Journal of Political Economy* 56: 23–34.

Carson, Jamie L., and Ryan J. Vander Wielen. 2002. "Partisan and Strategic Considerations in Conferee Selection in Congress." Paper presented at the Annual Meeting of the Midwest Political Science Association, Chicago.

Cassata, Donna. 1998. "Seeking Showdown with Clinton, Gingrich Gets One with GOP." *CQ Weekly* (March 14): 673.

Cochran, John. 2004. "Legislative Season Drawn in Solid Party Lines." *CQ Weekly* (January 3): 10–15.

Cox, Gary, and Mathew McCubbins. 2005. *Setting the Agenda: Responsible Party Gov-*

ernment in the US House of Representatives. Cambridge: Cambridge University Press.

Cox, Gary, and Mathew McCubbins. 2007. *Legislative Leviathan: Party Government in the House, 2nd Edition*. Cambridge: Cambridge University Press.

Cranford, John R. 1989. "Thrift Industry: 102 Conferees Appointed on S & L Bailout Bill." *CQ Weekly* (June 24): 1530.

Crook, Sara Brandes, and John R. Hibbing. 1985. "Congressional Reform and Party Discipline: The Effects of Changes in the Seniority System on Party Loyalty in the House of Representatives." *British Journal of Political Science* 15: 207–26.

Davidson, Roger H. 1981. "Subcommittee Government: New Channels for Policy Making." In *The New Congress*, ed. Thomas E. Mann and Norman J. Ornstein. Washington, DC: American Enterprise Institute.

Davidson, Roger H. 1989. "Multiple Referral of Legislation in the U.S. Senate." *Legislative Studies Quarterly* 14: 375–92.

Davidson, Roger H., Walter J. Oleszek, and Thomas Kephart. 1988. "One Bill, Many Committees: Multiple Referrals in the U.S. House of Representatives." *Legislative Studies Quarterly* 13: 3–28.

Deering, Christopher, and Steven S. Smith. 1997. *Committees in Congress, 3rd Edition*. Washington, DC: CQ Press.

Downs, Anthony. 1957. *An Economic Theory of Democracy*. New York: Harper.

Fenno, Richard F. 1966. *Power of the Purse: Appropriations Politics in Congress*. Boston: Little, Brown.

Fenno, Richard F. 1973. *Congressmen in Committees*. Boston: Little, Brown.

Ferejohn, John. 1975. "Who Wins in Conference Committee?" *Journal of Politics* 37: 1033–46.

Galloway, George B. 1953. *The Legislative Process in Congress*. New York: Thomas Y. Crowell.

Gamm, Gerald, and Steven S. Smith. Forthcoming. *Steering the Senate: The Development of Party Leadership in the U.S. Senate*. Cambridge: Cambridge University Press.

Glassman, Matthew Eric, and Sarah J. Eckman. 2015. "House Committee Party Ratios: 98th-114th Congresses." *Congressional Research Service: CRS Report R40478* (December 7).

Goldstein, Harvey, and Michael J. R. Healy. 1995. "The Graphical Presentation of a Collection of Means." *Journal of the Royal Statistical Society. Series A (Statistics in Society)* 158: 175–77.

Hansen, Ben B., Mark M. Fredrickson, Josh Buckner, Josh Errickson, and Peter Solenberger. 2016. "Package 'optmatch' Verson 0.9–6." https://cran.r-project.org/web/packages/optmatch/optmatch.pdf.

Hines, Eric H., and Andrew J. Civettini. 2004. "Conference Committee Appointments in the 101–107th Congresses." Paper presented at the Annual Meeting of the Iowa Political Science Association.

Ho, Daniel E., Kosuke Imai, Gary King, and Elizabeth A. Stuart. 2007. "Matching as Nonparametric Processing for Reducing Modeling Dependence in Parametric Causal Inference." *Political Analysis* 15: 199–236.

Ho, Daniel E., Kosuke Imai, Gary King, and Elizabeth A. Stuart. 2011. "MatchIt: Nonparametric Preprocessing for Parametric Causal Inference." *Journal of Statistical Software* 42:1–28.

Hulse, Carl. 2007. "In Conference: Process Undone by Partisanship." *New York Times* (September 26): 1.

Hurwitz, Mark S., Roger J. Moiles, and David W. Rohde. 2001. "Distributive and Partisan Issues in Agriculture Policy in the 104th House." *American Political Science Review* 95: 911–22.

Idelson, Holly. 1992. "Conference Tackles Huge Bill, but Thorniest Issues Remain." *CQ Weekly* (September 12): 2710–11.

Kady, Martin II. 2006. "Reid Will Be Quieter Hand at Senate's Helm." *CQ Weekly* (November 13): 2972.

King, David C. 1997. *Turf Wars: How Congressional Committees Claim Jurisdiction.* Chicago: University of Chicago Press.

Krehbiel, Keith. 1987. "Why Are Congressional Committees Powerful?" *American Political Science Review* 81: 929–35.

Krehbiel, Keith. 1991. *Information and Legislative Organization.* Ann Arbor: University of Michigan Press.

Lazarus, Jeffrey, and Nathan W. Monroe. 2007. "The Speaker's Discretion: Conference Committee Appointments from the 97th through 106th Congresses." *Political Research Quarterly* 60: 593–606.

Lee, Frances. 2016. *Insecure Majorities: Congress and the Perpetual Campaign.* Chicago: University of Chicago Press.

Longley, Lawrence D., and Walter J. Oleszek. 1989. *Bicameral Politics: Conference Committees in Congress.* New Haven: Yale University Press.

Lynch, Michael S., and Anthony J. Madonna. 2013. "Viva Voce: Implications of the Disappearing Voice Vote, 1865–1996." *Social Science Quarterly* 94: 530–50.

Maghsoodloo, Saeed, and Ching-Ying Huang. 2010. "Comparing the Overlapping of Two Independent Confidence Intervals with a Single Confidence Interval for Two Normal Population Parameters." *Journal of Statistical Planning and Inference* 140: 3295–3305.

Maltzman, Forrest. 1997. *Competing Principals: Committees, Parties, and the Organization of Congress.* Ann Arbor: University of Michigan Press.

Mayhew, David. 1991. *Divided We Govern.* New Haven: Yale University Press.

Mayhew, David. 2005. *Divided We Govern: Party Control, Lawmaking, and Investigations, 1946–2002.* 2nd edition. New Haven: Yale University Press.

McCown, Ada C. 1927. *The Congressional Conference Committee.* New York: Columbia University Press.

Nagler, Jonathan. 1989. "Strategic Implications of Conferee Selection in the House of Representatives." *American Politics Quarterly* 17: 54–79.

Oleszek, Walter J. 2008. "Whither the Role of Conference Committees: An Analysis." *Congressional Research Service: CRS Report 34611* (August 12).

Oleszek, Walter J., Mark J. Oleszek, Elizabeth Rybicki, and Bill Henniff Jr. 2016. *Congressional Procedures and the Policy Process.* 10th edition. Washington, DC: CQ Press.

Poole, Keith T., and Howard Rosenthal. 2007. *Ideology & Congress. Second, Revised Edition of Congress: A Political-Economic History of Roll Call Voting.* New Brunswick: Transaction Publishers.

Preston, Mark. 2004. "Conference Battle Escalates." *Roll Call* (February 2): http://www.rollcall.com/issues/49_71/-4172-1.html.

Poole, Keith T. 1998. "Recovering a Basic Space from a Set of Issue Scales." *American Journal of Political Science* 42: 954–93.

Rohde, David W. 1991. *Parties and Leaders in the Postreform House.* Chicago: University of Chicago Press.

Roberts, Jason M., Steven S. Smith, and Stephen R. Haptonstahl. 2016. "The Dimensionality of Congressional Voting Reconsidered." *American Politics Research* 44: 794–815.

Ryan, Josh M. 2011. "The Disappearing Conference Committee: The Use of Procedures by Minority Coalitions to Prevent Conferencing." *Congress & the Presidency* 38: 101–25.

Ryan, Josh M. 2014. "Conference Committee Proposal Rights and Policy Outcomes in the States." *Journal of Politics* 76: 1059–73.

Rybicki, Elizabeth. 2003. "Resolving Bicameral Differences in the U.S. Congress, 1789–2002." Paper presented at the Annual Meeting of the American Political Science Association, Philadelphia, PA.

Rybicki, Elizabeth. 2007. "The Development of Bicameral Resolution Procedures in the U.S. Congress." Ph.D. Dissertation. University of Minnesota.

Rybicki, Elizabeth. 2015. "Resolving Legislative Differences in Congress: Conference Committees and Amendments between the Houses." Congressional Research Service: CRS Report 98-696 (August 3).

Saturno, James V., and Jessica Tollestrup. 2015. "Omnibus Appropriations Acts: Overview of Recent Practices." *Congressional Research Service: CRS Report RL32473* (January 14).

Schick, Allen. 1980. *Congress and Money: Budgeting, Spending, and Taxing.* Washington, DC: Urban Institute.

Schickler, Eric, Eric McGhee, and John Sides. 2003. "Remaking the House and Senate: Personal Power, Ideology, and the 1970s Reforms." *Legislative Studies Quarterly* 28: 297–331.

Shepsle, Kenneth A., and Barry R. Weingast. 1987. "The Institutional Foundations of Committee Power." *American Political Science Review* 81: 85–104.

Sinclair, Barbara. 2012a. "Ping Pong and Other Congressional Pursuits: Party Leaders and Post-Passage Procedural Choice." In *Party and Procedure in the United States Congress,* ed. Jacob Strauss. Lanham, MD: Rowman and Littlefield.

Sinclair, Barbara. 2012b. *Unorthodox Lawmaking: New Legislative Process in the U.S. Congress, 4th ed.* Washington, DC: CQ Press.

Smith, Steven S. 1988. "As Essay on Sequence, Position, Goals, and Committee Power." *Legislative Studies Quarterly* 13: 151–76.

Smith, Steven S. 1989. *Call to Order: Floor Politics in the House and Senate.* Washington, DC: Brookings Institution.

Smith, Steven S. 2007. *Party Influence in Congress.* Cambridge: Cambridge University Press.

Smith, Seven S. 2014. *The Senate Syndrome: The Evolution of Parliamentary Warfare in the Modern U.S. Senate.* Norman: University of Oklahoma Press.

Smith, Steven S., and Gerald Gamm. 2009. "The Dynamics of Party Government in Congress." In *Congress Reconsidered, 9th Edition,* ed. Lawrence C. Dodd and Bruce I. Oppenheimer. Washington, DC: CQ Press.

Smith, Steven S., and Gerald Gamm. 2013. "The Dynamics of Party Government in Congress." In *Congress Reconsidered, 10th Edition*, ed. Lawrence C. Dodd and Bruce I. Oppenheimer. Washington, DC: CQ Press.

Steiner, Gilbert Yale. 1951. *The Congressional Conference Committee: Seventieth to Eightieth Congresses.* Urbana: University of Illinois Press.

Tiefer, Charles. 1989. *Congressional Practice and Procedure: A Reference, Research, and Legislative Guide.* New York: Greenwood Press.

Tsebelis, George, and Jeannette Money. 1997. *Bicameralism.* Cambridge: Cambridge University Press.

Van Beek, Stephen D. 1995. *Post-Passage Politics: Bicameral Resolution in Congress.* Pittsburgh: Pittsburgh University Press.

Van Houweling, Robert. 2006. "An Evolving End Game: The Partisan Use of Conference Committees, 1953–2003." In *Process, Party, and Policy Making: Further New Perspectives on the History of Congress*, ed. David Brady and Mathew McCubbins. Stanford: Stanford University Press.

Vander Wielen, Ryan J. 2006. "U.S. Congressional Conference Committees and Policy Outcomes." PhD diss., Washington University in St. Louis.

Vander Wielen, Ryan J. 2010. "The Influence of Conference Committees on Policy Outcomes." *Legislative Studies Quarterly* 25: 487–518.

Vander Wielen, Ryan J. 2012. "Why Conference Committees? A Theory of Conference Use in Structuring Bicameral Agreement." *Journal of Theoretical Politics* 25: 3–35.

Vander Wielen, Ryan J., and Steven S. Smith. 2011. "Majority Party Bias in U.S. Congressional Conference Committees." *Congress & the Presidency* 38: 271–300.

Vogler, David J. 1970. "Patterns of One House Dominance in Congressional Conference Committees." *Midwest Journal of Political Science* 14: 303–20.

Wolfensberger, Donald. 2008. "Have House-Senate Conferences Gone the Way of the Dodo?" *Roll Call* (April 28): 8.

Yoshinaka, Antoine. 2016. *Crossing the Aisle: Party Switching by U.S. Legislators in the Postwar Era.* Cambridge: Cambridge University Press.

Young, Garry, and Joseph Cooper. 1993. "Multiple Referral and the Transformation of House Decision Making." In *Congress Reconsidered, 5th Edition*, ed. Lawrence C. Dodd and Bruce I. Oppenheimer. Washington, DC: CQ Press.

Index

Note: Page numbers in *italics* refer to figures and tables.

Democratic Party (*continued*)
  factionalism among House Demo-
    crats, 19, 34–37, 63–64, 93, 125
  post-passage methods during 1980s
    and early 1990s, 40–41
  seat share in House and Senate, 12, *13*
  switching of conservatives to Republi-
    can Party, 20
  unseating of committee chairs, 20
  weakening of seniority system, 19–20
difference-in-difference (DID) analysis,
    162, 163
difference-of-means tests, 150, *153*, 153–
    56, *154*, *155*, *156*
distribution of policy preferences. *See*
    partisan polarization
divided party control
  appropriations legislation affected by,
    100–102
  defense authorization legislation
    affected by, 119
  increase in, 123, 131
  partisan competition affected by, 14
  polarization effects, 17–18
  stalemate expectations, 48
  tax legislation conflict, 117–18
Dole, Bob, 42
don't ask, don't tell policy, 119
DW-NOMINATE scores
  for conference committee bias mea-
    surement, 71–72
  in five policy domains, 94, *95*
  for standing committee bias measure-
    ment, 57

electronic voting, 23–24, *24*
emergency legislation, 17–18, 100
energy bill conference (1992), 40
Ethics committees, majority seats on,
    166n3
exchange of amendments
  for appropriations legislation, 105
  defined, xii, 3
  interaction with cloture votes, 46–47
  post-conference stage, 149
  rules limiting, 165n1
  in second wave of post-passage
    changes, 45–46
  types of, 32

explanatory statements of conference
    proceedings, 128, 144, 145, 170n26
ex post veto model, 10

Federal Aid to Education Act (1960), 134
filibuster
  campaign finance reform filibuster,
    44, 135
  conference reports, 147
  defense authorization legislation, 119,
    120
  increasing use of, 28, 42
  reforms of 2013, 44, 47, 135
  related to conferences, 43–44, 129
  strategic challenges for, 14
filling the amendment tree, 46–47
Finance committees, 85, 114
first wave of post-passage changes
  decline in conference committees, xii,
    32–34, *33*
  effect on bias in conferences, 68,
    70–71
  factionalism among House Demo-
    crats, 34–37, 63–64, 93, 125
  integration of policy making, 37–40
fiscal cliff, 113, 122
fiscal policy legislation
  challenges to committee-based exper-
    tise, 127
  expectations of greater change in, 97
  matching analysis on, 156, 161–63,
    162
  party interest in, 85
  role in post-passage politics, 91–92,
    123, 125
  See also appropriations legislation;
    budget legislation; tax legislation
floor amendments, 23–24, *24*
Foley, Thomas, 40
Food and Agriculture Act (1965), 121
Food for Peace program, 121
food stamp program, 121, 122
fractional advantages in committee seats
    and conference delegations
  bias from, 71, 82, 84, *84t*
  effect from two waves of change, 70
  evidence of, 67, 69, *69t*
  multivariate estimates, 58, 87, 89
Freedom Caucus, 113